A Reed Shaken by the Wind

Gavin Maxwell was born in 1914. In 1945 he bought the small Hebridean island of Soay and tried to establish a shark fishery. This resulted in his first book *Harpoon at a Venture*. *God Protect Me from My Friends*, a biography of Salvatore Giuliano, appeared in 1956, followed by *A Reed Shaken by the Wind* (1957) and *The Ten Pains of Death* (1959), a study of a Sicilian peasant community. In 1960 his most famous book, *Ring of Bright Water*, was published, of which there are more than a million copies in print in English. In this engrossing and beautifully written autobiography he describes his pioneering days in Camusfeàrna in the Western Highlands, and introduces his beloved otters, Mijbil and Edal. A sequel, *The Rocks Remain* (1963), records his travels in North Africa and his subsequent joyful return to Camusfeàrna. *The House of Elrig* (1965) is the personal story of Gavin Maxwell's childhood and boyhood in the isolated moorlands of Galloway, and shows how his love of wild land and creatures was formed. *Raven Seek Thy Brother*, his last book published in 1968, combines a description of Camusfeàrna with his own biography. *The Otters' Tale*, an abridged and pictorial children's version of *Ring of Bright Water*, appeared in 1962. He also wrote *Lords of the Atlas* (1966), a history of the Moroccan House of Glaoua. Several of his books are published in Penguin. Gavin Maxwell died in 1969.

In the early part of 1956 Gavin Maxwell accompanied the famous explorer, Wilfred Thesiger, on a journey to the unexplored marshlands of southern Iraq. *A Reed Shaken by the Wind* is the absorbing account of the people he met and his experiences during his travels in this remote area. It also tells how he acquired his first otter, Mijbil, who proved to be of a race previously unknown to science and later christened by zoologists as *Lutrogale perspicillata maxwelli*, or Maxwell's otter.

GAVIN MAXWELL

A REED SHAKEN BY THE WIND

Be sure this land of nowhere will expel
All those who seek a chance outlandish spell
That any place could offer just as well.

PENGUIN BOOKS

Penguin Books Ltd, Harmondsworth, Middlesex, England
Penguin Books, 625 Madison Avenue, New York, New York 10022, U.S.A.
Penguin Books Australia Ltd, Ringwood, Victoria, Australia
Penguin Books Canada Ltd, 2801 John Street, Markham, Ontario, Canada L3R 1B4
Penguin Books (N.Z.) Ltd, 182–190 Wairau Road, Auckland 10, New Zealand

First published by Longmans, Green and Co. Ltd 1957
Published in Penguin Books 1983

Made and printed in Great Britain
by Richard Clay (The Chaucer Press) Ltd,
Bungay, Suffolk

For M. M.

Τροφεῖα

Author's Note

THIS book is the story of a journey through an almost unknown land, and my first thanks are due to Wilfred Thesiger for allowing me to travel with him into his private paradise.

Secondly to the only other European who shares much of Thesiger's knowledge. He first towered on my horizon as a namesake against whose memory the Arabs measured me to my discredit, as a man who could shave with three strokes of a razor and had learned their language in a week. To him, Gavin Young, I owe much for help in avoiding technical inaccuracies in the manuscript.

To all the Iraqis, from the highest to the lowest who showed almost unvarying kindness, courtesy, and hospitality, go my respectful salutations and warm gratitude; and in apology for quoting the efforts of a few to speak my language I would add that I think they must have found my attempts at theirs as funny.

Having a particular ennui for the type of travel book that reads "The people do not build houses; they live (*hudl*) in tents (*riz*) which they fold up (*slamm*) when they want to move (*scipp*) . . ." I have avoided using Arabic words except where they are strictly necessary; it would in any case be a presumption on the part of one who knows as little of the language as I. For terms that are of real importance the serious student may refer to Wilfred Thesiger's deeply informative contribution to the *Journal of the Royal Central Asian Society*, January 1954, from which its author and the Society have kindly allowed me to quote two passages and to base my map upon his.

For reasons that will not require explanation it has seemed undesirable to give to all characters their true names, and thus it has appeared pointless to include an index to a book which is, perhaps, in any case too much of a personal narrative to merit one.

I am indebted to the following for permission to quote copyright material: Mr. Alan Hodge for an extract from his poem "The World of Nowhere"; Messrs. Hamish Hamilton, Ltd. for an extract from "The Journey", from *Collected Poems* by Kathleen Raine; the Editor of *New Statesman and Nation* for an extract from "Death of a Rat" by Anthony Thwaite, which appeared in the 8 September, 1956 issue of *New Statesman and Nation*; and Mr. Wilfrid Thesiger and the Royal Central Asian Society for material from the January 1954 issue of the *Journal of the Royal Central Asian Society*.

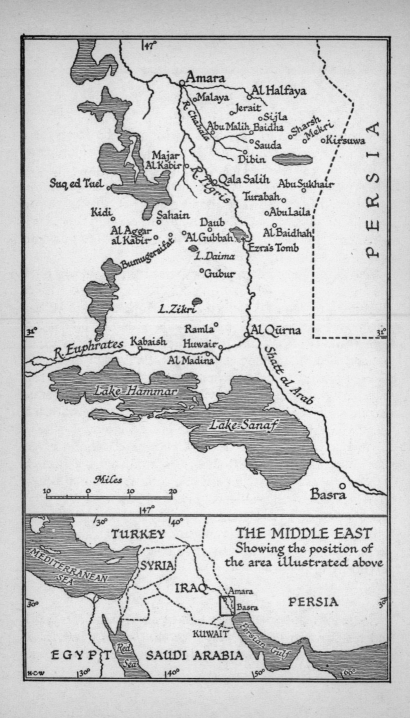

THE MIDDLE EAST
Showing the position of
the area illustrated above

Prologue

WE seemed to have been flying over the desert for a very long time. I could remember no beginning to it and there seemed no end; it stretched away everywhere to a horizon that was smoky and dim with the approach of evening. The dipping sun defined the slopes and ridges of the dunes, and we were low enough to see here and there small huddles of black Bedouin tents, but nowhere was there a glint of water.

The passenger in front of me passed the flight log over his shoulder. Speed 220 m.p.h., altitude 5,000, ETA Baghdad 2145 hours. I looked at my companion, but he was asleep and I didn't think these details would be interesting enough to warrant waking him. I passed the slip of paper on, and went on looking at the desert. Every now and again I could make out specks whose shadows were longer than themselves, long rows of moving specks that were the camel caravans of the nomads. They and the clusters of black tents were the only signs of life in all the desert.

As I looked down at them I became conscious of an emotion, an unease, and I shrugged it off, but it returned, demanding attention. I took it and looked at it and turned it over, as it were, and recognised it with surprise, even bewilderment. I was feeling afraid. Beside me Wilfred Thesiger, more at home among the black tents and camels of the Bedouin than in his native country and among his own people, slept on.

Some two and a half years before, in September 1954, I had read an article by Thesiger in the *Journal of the Royal Geographical Society*. Thesiger is famous as a traveller in

Arabia, one of the first men to have mapped the Empty Quarter, the great stretch of unoccupied desert that forms the south-east interior of the Arabian peninsula. This article had been called "The Marshmen of Southern Iraq", and it described the life of a primitive and previously unexplored people among whom Thesiger had spent some months of each year since 1950. They lived, it seemed, hidden in a watery waste of marsh and lagoon untravelled by any early explorer, dwelling in reed huts built upon little floating islands like dabchicks' nests.

"The Ma'dan," he wrote, "have acquired an evil name. The aristocratic tribes despise them for their dubious lineage, and willingly impute to them every sort of perfidy and wickedness, while the townsmen fear them, shun them and readily believe all that they hear against them. Among the British, too, their reputation is bad, a legacy from the First World War when from the shelter of their marshes they murdered and looted both sides indiscriminately as opportunity offered. . . . They have a well-established reputation as thieves, but have not, as yet, stolen anything from me. . . . Hard and primitive, their way of life has endured for centuries, but in the next few years the marshes will be drained and the marshmen as I have known them will disappear to be merged into the stereotype pattern of the modern world —more comfortable, perhaps, but certainly less free and less picturesque. Like many others, I regret the forces which are inexorably suburbanising the untamed places and turning tribesmen into corner boys."

When I read this article I had been searching for somewhere to go, somewhere that was not already suburbanised and where there was still something left to see that had not already been seen and described by hundreds or thousands of my kind before me. The margins of the atlas were closing in; the journeys I had dreamed in years before were blocked by the spreading stains of new political empires and impenetrable frontiers behind which, if propaganda is to be believed, the suburbanising process progressed but the faster.

I wrote to Thesiger, who was in London for the autumn and early winter, and we arranged to meet. He was very unlike the preconceived theories I had held about his appearance. The knowledge of his years of primitive living in the Sudan, Ethiopia, and Arabia, of ordeals and hardships past, had led me, perhaps, to expect someone a little indifferent to his personal appearance, someone with a contempt for conformity to the conventions of a European social group. The bowler hat, the hard collar and black shoes, the never-opened umbrella, all these were a surprise to me.

He was willing enough that I should accompany him when he returned to his marshes in January, but doubtful of my ability to stand the discomfort of the life.

"You seem to have led a fairly rough life," he said, "but this would be a bit different from anything you've had before. Can you sleep on the hard ground all right?—because you won't see a mattress in the marshes."

I told him that I was well accustomed to it.

"And insect bites. The fleas there can be really quite something. They don't happen to bite me, but sometimes they keep me awake by sheer weight of numbers, and the Arabs themselves are often driven half crazy by them."

Any flea within a mile's radius finds me and falls on me as though famished; they walk about me munching as they go, leaving red mountains with long connecting ridges between them. I thought it better not to mention this for the moment.

"And then there's diseases. The marsh people have every disease you can think of and lots that you can't—practically all infectious. It's my hobby; I'm not a trained doctor, but one acquires knowledge through experience and necessity. One tries to do something for them, and you'll find that we spend a lot of time doctoring. I've built up a certain immunity, but I don't know how you'd get on. They've all got

3

dysentery, you know, and as the water level round their houses fluctuates the drinking supply and the public lavatory become one and the same thing. I took one Englishman into the marshes and he was carried out after ten days two stone lighter than he came in. He'd have died if I hadn't sent him back."

I was determined to let nothing stand between me and this opportunity, and I professed complete indifference to all diseases. He had one more try. "I wonder how long you can sit cross-legged. I'm always on the move, rarely spend two nights in the same place, and we travel in a canoe. So a great deal of every day is spent sitting cross-legged in the bottom of it. And you'll find that when you are ashore you spend a lot more time cross-legged on the floor of a marshman's hut. Can you sit cross-legged?"

I said I could try.

"Well," said Thesiger, "if you're so determined to come I'll be glad to have you with me." And so it was arranged.

But it was not to be as easy as all that. I couldn't get the necessary visas. For weeks I found myself positively fighting to reach the fleas and diseases and hardships, but it was a losing battle, and at length Thesiger left without me. I returned to Sicily, where I had spent part of the two previous years, and scratched disconsolately at Sicilian fleas and had a bout of inferior Sicilian dysentery, and mourned the rich and varied ailments of the Promised Land. I told my Sicilian friends of my disappointment, and they, whose dream world was of tiled bathrooms and chromium plating, were incredulous.

"*Mamma mia! Perchê?*" they cried. "Why did you want to go to this terrible place?" I said it was better than shooting big game in Africa, but I had forgotten that this was a strictly British joke, and nobody understood.

The summer passed in the burning dusty heat of a Sicilian

4

village, and in autumn I came back to London, to rain and lights reflected in wet black streets.

In January I met Thesiger several times, but by now my commitments appeared so interminable that there could be no hope of leaving the country again before April. He himself was returning to the marshes at the end of January, and on the twenty-third, his last free evening before leaving, we dined together again.

"It's a pity you weren't able to come last year," he said, "because there won't be another chance. I feel I've had long enough there, and this is my last journey. I'm leaving the marshes in April, and I shall spend the summer among the pastoral tribes before going on to Afghanistan. You could join me in April, if you like, for a couple of months, but of course the life isn't as different from anything else as life in the marshes is."

I leapt at that invitation, and we parted sometime after midnight, with a rendezvous in Basra on April the second.

When I got home I found that I couldn't sleep. At first I thought I was restless at the prospect, however far off, of a journey to which I looked forward, but as after an hour or two the cigarette ends in the ashtray grew more numerous and more like a squalid family of white grubs, I understood that my discontent was because Thesiger was going to the marshes for the last time and I was staying behind in London. I was passing up an opportunity which could not be repeated. "You could never go there alone unless you spoke their dialect," he had said. "There won't be another chance."

Decisions greater than this are made with no more logic or forethought. By four o'clock in the morning I had made up my mind and I went to sleep.

I was awake by seven-thirty, and the hour before I thought I could reasonably telephone to Thesiger seemed very long. He answered the telephone himself.

"Wilfred—if I can get the visas, can I come with you on Monday?"

There was a moment's silence at the other end.

"I thought you were so busy you couldn't leave London before April! Monday would be pretty short notice for someone who wasn't busy at all. Are you serious?"

"Quite serious. I'll arrange everything somehow. All right?"

"All right. The plane leaves at 9.50, flight No. 770. I'll be starting from Victoria at 7.45. Better dine with me here first. I'll expect you at half-past six."

"What about luggage?"

"You don't want any luggage. There isn't room to carry it in the marshes anyway. Take two shirts, two pairs of trousers and a jacket. One pair of shoes. Something that kicks off easily, because you have to take them off every time you go into a house." (I didn't know that the same shoes would have to stay on in the clinging grip of soft clay.) "And a razor. That's all. Take what you like as far as Basra, if you want more. We can comb it out and leave the inessentials there."

"When shall I see you?"

"Dinner on the night we leave. Good-bye."

At the end of four hectic days there was no certainty that I should get visas for the tribal areas. I had a normal visa to spend three months in the country, and a request to call upon the Minister of Public Relations in Baghdad.

The plane droned on over the Syrian desert towards Baghdad.

Chapter One

I HAD no very clear preconceived picture of Baghdad, and my experience of Arab towns had been limited to brief sojourns in North Africa. My first impression was that what the western colonial powers could do to a city in the way of desecration was nothing to what the Arabs themselves could do when they got going. And they had got going, with all the revenue of the oil fields behind their enthusiasm.

It is perhaps the least favourable time for many centuries for a stranger to see Baghdad; the moment of transition from an eastern to a western culture that has as yet little true meaning for the bulk of the people.

I have noticed that there is a longitudinal line east of which the squalor created by building appears as great as that of demolition. Buildings were going up everywhere, bleak blocks in the western tradition, whose desolate uniformity was increased by the veneer of dust and the rubble from which they grew; new roads and streets were everywhere under construction, and pale dust clung to the palm trees and tarnished their leaves. Dotted between the new roads and the new houses, and covered too with the dust of their construction, were mud houses and reed matting houses, but everywhere except where the traffic was thick lay litter and refuse, and everywhere the black kites wheeled on the bare sky overhead. Gleaming Cadillacs painted in fantastic colours blared their horns at ragged Arabs riding side-saddle on limping donkeys. Every possible permutation and combination between pure Arab clothes and pure European jostled the street, but the national garb is on its way out. European clothes are the official dress of Iraq, and in the towns anything else is equated with lack of education.

Unchanged through this noisy apostasy from tradition flow the broad and splendid waters of the Tigris, spanned only by three or four ugly iron bridges of British construction. Along its western bank are many of the old Turkish houses built round a tiled and mosaic courtyard, in whose gardens are trees where small pastel-shaded doves cluster on the branches like delicately bloomed fruit. But the Turkish houses, much in demand by British residents in Baghdad, are condemned. To the Iraqis, with gold in their hands and impatient for development, they seem archaic and unfunctional.

"They have only two words for everything," said Thesiger, "*moderne* and *demodé*, and what isn't the first is the second."

Of the eight million people who live within the frontiers of Iraq, Baghdad now holds over a million, and more pour into the city every day. Except in the remote tribal areas the children now receive a school education, and as a result consider themselves too good to work on the land; indeed land work is considered to be the lowest of all occupations. So, hearing of great wealth in the cities—the picture thus presented being no clearer, perhaps, than it would have been five centuries ago—a youth will leave his home and drift to Baghdad. Here, to avoid loss of face, he will acquire European clothes, and these, being according to his means, are often already ragged and disreputable. If he is lucky he will find work at the equivalent of five shillings a day, but when it rains all employment stops automatically, and he is dependent on what he may earn by more dubious means. Thus juvenile delinquency is said to be practically universal, and after dark the streets are haunted by skulking striplings ready to grab or earn a coin by any means at their disposal.

Mass evils of this kind are perhaps inherent in any change as rapid and complete as comes to those countries where oil, the raw material of western industrial civilisation, is to be

8

found; but it is nevertheless a sorry moment in which to visit the oldest culture in the world, the country that taught the ancient Egyptians to write. It is a *fin d'époque*, bringing with it corruption, unrest and bewilderment, of which only the highest level, that which has been educated for generations, is free. The town Iraqi now want one thing and one thing only, the American Way of Life, and the bulk of the people have as yet little realisation that this implies more than a multiplicity of sophisticated automatic toys, for some eighty per cent of the population of all Iraq is still illiterate. After four days in Baghdad I found myself remembering again Thesiger's phrase: "tribesmen into corner boys".

In Rashid Street, the Piccadilly of Baghdad, I tried to buy the standard primer of the language, Van Ess's *Spoken Arabic of Iraq*. In the bookshop an Iraqi girl with a lot of make-up told me in English that it was out of stock, but produced another with a similar title, which she said was much more highly thought of. This I bought, but it was not until after some days of utter bewilderment that I discovered that it was intended to be used in conjunction with gramophone records.

"You are walking alone," I read. "You want to talk to someone, so you talk to a young Baghdadi. You tell him 'good evening', and he replies. Then you say that you are an American and tell him your name. He is glad to know you and tells you his name is Said. You tell him you have just come to Iraq. You add that your friend came with you. You say your father has a farm near New York, and you work in a big automobile factory. And you want to work in the factory when you go back to America. While you are talking, Said's friend Hassan comes up to you. . . . Said asks Hassan where he is going. Hassan says to the King Ghazi movie. It's a good movie, he says." I flicked over a few pages. "Father I want to introduce these Americans to you; this is

9

John and this is his friend Bill. John's from New York but Bill's from Texas." *Father:* "My oldest son went to America. He's an American now." ... "You have been introduced to an Iraqi named Ali. He asks where you are from. You say you are an American and tell him what part you came from. ... You ask him if he knows Ford cars. Yes, he says, Ford cars are good, in fact he has one. He says there is a Ford factory in Baghdad. ... Later you are walking around with Ali. Ali calls your attention to another man. What is his work, you ask. Ali says he doesn't work; he is a merchant and has a big shop in the market. You ask Ali if he knows him. Ali says yes, and he also knows his son. His son doesn't work much either, he likes to walk around all the time."

Oh, Arabian Nights; oh, Christopher Columbus; oh, Tree of Knowledge of Good and Evil.

The Minister was gracious and affable. He thanked us for our courtesy in calling upon him, which, he said, was of course completely unnecessary, as Iraq was a free country and foreigners could travel where they wished. He touched on the problems of the expanding city. "All Iraq is coming to Baghdad," he said. "Here they have everything they want; every boy has a wireless set, every girl a sewing machine. They leave the country for the towns as though they were running from an epidemic. We couldn't stop them coming if we wanted to." He armed Thesiger with letters to the Governors of the provinces in which we should be travelling, and that night we left by train for Basra.

Of Basra, the greatest port of the Persian Gulf, I had as fleeting and necessarily as superficial an impression as of Baghdad. Here, though the present Basra is not an ancient city, the old and the new, the east and the west, seemed even more inextricably woven, for the very new of the gleaming traffic and the concrete buildings is set against a middle distance, rather than a far background, of primitive life.

We lived in the most modern quarter of Basra, Ashar—and during my short stay I saw little of any other—at a Consulate-General worthy to be an embassy, as the guest of a Consul-General worthy to be an ambassador. Beyond the green and gracious walled garden lay a broad street and then the great river, the Shatt al Arab, which is the fusion of the Tigris and the Euphrates in their last miles to the sea. Palms fringed the farther bank, and on its surface rowed, paddled, roared, stammered, or simply drifted, craft of every conceivable description. Big Arab trading boats under full sail, primitive bitumen-coated canoes from the waterways surrounding the marshes, motor launches and passenger paddle steamers, naval vessels, big ocean-going merchantmen, and completely circular rafts carrying loads of reed matting from the marshlands, drifting downstream without propulsion; the paths of all these were woven together like a tableau representing the history of surface craft.

The clothing of the people who crowded the streets was as diverse as the boats upon the river, but I began to understand the various grades, as it were, of dress in Iraq, and their social significance. There is only one reasonably constant factor, and that is the head-dress. Non-Europeanised Iraqis wear their hair shaven to a short stubble, and over it a skull cap, often bright or multi-coloured with floral design, oversewn into a quilted pattern. The skull cap, however, is usually hidden, except in the case of children, by the loose, turban-like *keffia* which is worn over it. The formal *keffia* in Iraq is white with a black pattern on it, like Rylock wire netting, and signifies that the wearer belongs to the Shi'a sect of Muslims, those who believe the Prophet's son-in-law and cousin Ali to have been his rightful successor, and after him his two sons Hassan and Hussain. The first of these was murdered by his wife, and the other, driven by a frantic belief in his own cause, died a martyr's death in battle, backed by flames that he had lit to cut off his own retreat. His tomb at Kerbela, and that of Ali at Nejef, are the two great places of pilgrimage for the Shi'a sect. (The Shi'a and the Sunni, who preponderate outside the frontiers of Iraq and Persia, are the two great divisions of the Muslim world, the Sunni originating as followers of the Prophet's uncle Abu Bakr. Sunni means, in a broad sense, "orthodox", and Shi'a "partisan".)

The headcloth may be worn loosely draped over the head and shoulders or it may be wound up and tied into the shape of a turban; in either case it is held in place by a headrope or *agal*, two snake-like black twists fitting on to the crown of the head. The *agal* is like the top two coils of a weak spring, wooden at the core, and bound over with black wool. There are variations of the head-dress as there are of everything else; the very poor or primitive often wear no *agal*, and the *keffia* itself may be no more than a rag of any colour knotted round the head.

But it is below the neck that the diversity of garments becomes really confusing. Basically, there is a single prototype of all the elaborations, a simple shirt reaching from the throat to the feet, like a nightgown, of any sober colour except black, and sometimes striped like pyjamas. This is the *dish-dasha* worn by all poorer people who have not yet adopted European clothes, but in cooler weather it is now quite customary to wear over this an ordinary European jacket. With or without this jacket the outer layer may be worn, a cloak or *bisht*, black, brown, or dark blue. It is never thick; in its crudest form it is loosely woven of hard, hairless brown wool and it is unornamented, but it may, among the more elegant, be diaphanous as fine muslin, and often carries an edging of gold braid and gold tassels.

The next stage beyond the simple *dish-dasha*, among the well-to-do who do not wear trousers, is, broadly speaking, a coat and skirt of dark cloth. The coat is rather longer and fuller than is customary in Europe, and the ground length

skirt continues upward as a wrap-round dress, to form a V
at the chest like that of an ordinary waistcoat. Above this
V appears a shirt, but rarely a collar or tie, giving a somewhat unfinished appearance to an ambitious scheme. This is
the customary wear of the sheikhs and other unwesternised
people of importance. With it go black towny-looking
shoes, but seldom socks. The poor people are always barefoot.

I went to the *suq* to buy a belt. With recollections of
North African *suq*, and that of Marrakesh in particular, I had
expected quarters of leather-workers, gold-workers, silver-
workers, rug sellers; all the enticements of beautiful and
exotic goods. I crossed a wooden bridge over a canal
cluttered with all types of boats and of Asiatic humanity. A
negro in a knee-length *dish-dasha* clutched my arm and thrust
a packet of postcards under my nose. They were, I saw, of
another large negro posturing indecently in a very expensive
looking bedroom. As I brushed them away he instantly
substituted a second packet. The top photograph was so
excruciatingly funny that had I been in a less public place I
should have asked to see the rest. A bulgy semitic woman of
uncertain age, naked but for a pair of very high-heeled shoes,
posed with grotesque coquettishness against a painted back-
cloth of palms and minarets. Both hands were raised, one to
shoulder level and the other curved high above her head in
a parody of sinuous grace. From under coal-black eyelids
she ogled the camera with a perceptible squint; but the
beauty of the picture lay in what she was holding. Draped
from her two upraised hands hung a thin rope-like length of
black silk, cunningly screening from view every part of her
body that would have been hidden by a modern two-piece
bathing dress. I wondered whether these photographs were
much in demand among the Arabs, for they could hardly
have been calculated to call forth a frenzy of lust from a
visiting European.

I entered the *suq* and walked between lines of stalls selling aluminium pots and pans, cheap Japanese china, bales of bright coloured Indian cotton, and fibreware luggage. Everything either came from Europe or was a further-eastern imitation of western commodities. At last I stopped a particularly European-looking Iraqi and asked him if he spoke English. Enough, he said; so I asked him if he could tell me where to buy a leather belt. "Leather?" he said. "I suppose it is possible. But why not plastic? It is much better. We all use plastic now; all the shops have plastic belts. Cheaper, better."

Wandering on through the *suq* I came at length to a quarter of so deafening a din that I realised that here at last was something actually being made. It sounded like hundreds of men hitting sheets of metal with hammers; and that was precisely what it was, sheets of aluminium being made into household utensils, and sheets of copper being fashioned into a particular shape of coffee pot that is standard throughout all Iraq. On that first visit it was the only evidence of any local industry that I discovered. I did in the end return with a leather belt, but on its inner surface was stamped in Roman letters the words "Made in Germany".

Three out of Thesiger's four canoe boys had arrived to meet us in Basra. In those days when I did not know them I found their presence acutely embarrassing. At the Consulate-General Thesiger and I shared a huge bedroom. After my excursion to the *suq* Thesiger was nowhere about, and I sat down in an arm-chair to look at a map. After a few moments the door opened silently and the three canoe boys entered. I said good afternoon, which was about all I could say. They returned my greeting and sat down cross-legged on the floor, in a semicircle round my feet. All three stared at me without the least expression. Each dangled from his fingers a string of beads, one red, one yellow, and one white. The beads clicked slowly and rhythmically, my watch ticked, and if I looked up those six eyes still looked un-waveringly into my face. If I met any of their eyes indivi-dually they would glance away, but as I looked down again at the map they would come back to my face. I tried smiling at them, and they smiled back, but with anticipation, as though I were now about to say something, which I could not. I had already found out that my few words of North African Arabic were unintelligible.

Amara, Hassan, and Sabeti; Kathia, the fourth, was to join us a day or two later when we began our journey. Both in feature and in character they were as unlike as they could be; they had little in common but the colour of skins. Amara was a handsome self-possessed youth of eighteen, fine boned, disdainful as an Arab stallion, often moody and with-drawn. He alone of them seemed always at ease in the sur-roundings of civilisation; there could never be anything gauche or awkward in his movements or in his response to an unfamiliar situation. At this time his natural vanity pre-occupied much of his attention on his newly growing moustache and beard, at whose infinitesimal length he would snip, absorbed, with a pair of nail scissors. He liked mirrors.

Hassan was a year or two older, a bouncing but volatile extravert with peculiarly heavy eyebrows and just-noticeably underhung jaw. He and Sabeti, both of whom were married, were the most habitually good-humoured of the four, but Sabeti's good humour was of a different quality, something almost pathological; he was the type of the Family Slave. If there was any odd job to be done it was naturally Sabeti who did it; his desire to serve and to please seemed as if it must have been developed in compensation for a total absence of looks or charm. Sabeti looked like an apologetic crow, and the wide eyebrow-moustache that he wore did not succeed in any way in altering the essentially placatory character of his face.

The map at which I looked while the three looked at me

was so blank as to be scarcely worthy of the name. There were rivers, tributaries and distributaries, and great areas covered with a small tufted symbol to represent marsh. To a few place-names, very widely scattered, someone had added a question mark in red ink, and in some cases drawn a red line clean through them. This was the area of permanent marshland to which we were going, and the bulk of it lay some forty miles north and west of Basra. Some two-thirds of the way across it the Tigris ran from north to south, vertically, so to speak, while the Euphrates ran horizontally from the west to form the southern boundary.

As recently as Biblical times the Persian Gulf stretched far up the country that is now known as Iraq. The two great rivers, the Tigris and the Euphrates, flowed separately into the sea; not, as they do now, through the common conduit of the Shatt al Arab on whose banks Basra stands. As the sea receded it left in its wake a country of marshes, creeks and lagoons, which was settled in earliest times by immigrants from the Persian and Turkish Highlands. The living conditions of these earliest settlers differed very little from those of the marshmen of today; their reed houses and their few possessions have been excavated at the level just above the virgin silt.

As the centuries went by, the great area of marshland exposed by the sea became divided into areas of seasonal flooding, semi-permanent marshlands; and, fed by the many distributaries of the two great rivers, a central area of permanent marsh which exists to this day. These permanent marshes lie low between the courses of the two great rivers, and extend east of the Tigris over the Persian frontier. The farther the sea has receded the farther south has become the area which is at all times of the year without solid ground, and until Thesiger came there in 1950 it has remained one of the unexplored territories nearest to civilisation. Whereas the areas of seasonal flooding, the great rivers themselves, and the fringes of the permanent marsh, have all been visited both by travellers and by armies in wars of European origin, the heart of the marshes and its people have remained unknown.

It was, I had learned from Thesiger's article, a tribal area inhabited by some half dozen tribes whose frontiers extended arbitrarily outside the marshes. Some of them claimed to be not of Arab descent, while others contained a liberal sprinkling of *Sayids*, or linear descendants of the Prophet. The generic name for the marshmen is Ma'dan, a term used to define not a tribe but a way of life; the people who have for many centuries been proficient in extracting their livelihood from a waste land of water and of reeds, and who have had little or no contact with the world outside.

Because the physical geography of the country has been in such constant change it is difficult to trace the origins of the Ma'dan with any certainty. The marshes were very much farther north when the first immigrants came from the east to settle there, and that was more than five thousand years ago; during the Dark Ages there were other happenings besides the successive conquests of the Medes, Persians, Greeks, Romans, and finally the Arabs, that may well have added stranger blood to that of the marshmen. In the early part of the ninth century A.D. bands of robber gipsies settled in the marshes. After a while, their numbers increased by malcontents and refugees from justice, these became proclaimed rebels against the Caliph, who found this petty insurrection so difficult to quell that he was taunted with being unable to catch a few hundred frogs within arm's reach of him. They capitulated at last, but it seems that those who could remain among the reeds did so, mistrusting the promise of amnesty should they emerge.

Some fifty years after this, in 869, there began a rebellion which for nearly fourteen years shook all Southern Iraq, and which seemed, indeed, as if it would throw out the Arabs and lead to a negro empire in the east.

The confusion that had succeeded the death of the

Prophet in A.D. 633, and the strife over the dubious succession, was still at that time fruitful ground for exploitation by any unscrupulous claimant. More difficult was the amassing of a following strong enough to enforce the claim.

In the two hundred and fifty years since Mahommed's death his *soi disant* linear descendants had become legion, and there was, therefore, nothing original in the fact of a certain Ali ibn Mahommed, a man from near the modern city of Teheran, giving himself out to be of the blood of the Prophet; nor in his early unsuccessful attempts to gain influence in various communities where existing schism offered a foothold for opportunism. He failed in Basra—a town standing farther to the west than the present city of the same name—and was forced to flee to Baghdad, but not long afterward he returned to the south with quite a different plan in mind. He had chosen for his raw material of rebellion the mass of African slaves who were called Zenj, men of the country now known as Zanzibar.

Huge numbers of these slaves were occupied on the waste land that lay to the east of Basra, engaged in digging away the surface stratum of soil, rich in profitable saltpetre, and at the same time exposing the cultivable layer beneath it. Their work was of the hardest, and their living of the meanest, for here was none of the affection and tolerance that can grow between the master and the slave who is attached to one family or household. In these men who hated all but their own kind, Ali—"the Abominable One", as he came to be called—saw the strength and ferocity that should sweep him to power.

His approach to the slaves reveals a cynical acumen, a deep psychological insight, worthy of any later propagandist. He spoke to them with the tongues of God and of Mammon, so that the two images became for them inextricably confused. The religious sect to which he proclaimed allegiance—inconsistently with his alleged descent from the Prophet's daughter—would appear to have been chosen solely for one of its slogans: that the ruler should be the best man ."even though he were an Ethiopian slave". To that sect, the Kharijites, the deadliest of all sins was failure to acknowledge themselves as the true representatives of Islam. All other Muslims, therefore, they might dutifully destroy as infidels.

That was clearly the doctrine most likely to appeal to the slaves in their bitterness, and on the worldly side he preached not the right of equality with their overlords but their right to own slaves themselves.

The revolt of the slaves under the leadership of Ali the Abominable began in September 869, and almost immediately their headquarters came to be the marshlands surrounding the Tigris. Their tactics were night attack and ambush of their suppressors' boats from the screening reed beds. There were at first some fifty thousand men, but their army was swelled by Bedouin and malcontents of every description, and when the rebellion showed early promise of success many black soldiers of the Caliph deserted and went over to Ali. Within a year they had built a city on the west bank of the Tigris, from which they raided and plundered towns far afield, even invading Khuzistan to the east of the Persian frontier. After capture or partial destruction of any city Ali would parade before the survivors the heads of the dead; when in 871 he finally captured Basra itself the lowest estimate of these was 300,000, and the slaves waded in the blood of the free men whom they had butchered. By 879 the power of the Zenj was at its greatest; they had by now captured many of the cities of Babylonia, and even part of Kurdistan had surrendered to them. But they garrisoned and held little if any of their conquests, returning always to the marshlands in which lay their permanent safety.

In 881, twelve years after the insurrection, the war entered upon its final phase, the siege of the city that the rebel slaves had built. Mokhtara, "the city of the elect", they called it, but their enemies spoke of it as The Abominable

City. At the beginning of the siege it was said to have contained 300,000 fighting men, and a negro king who ruled over them.

The city withstood two years' siege, and when at last it fell in 883 the King of the Zenj had fled from it, and it was the head of Ali the Abominable himself that was laid at the feet of the Caliph's besieging general. It has been suggested that he died by his own hand, in the ruins of his city, for no man came forward to claim the fabulous reward.

Many of the Zenj who escaped from the city fought on from the reedy thickets of the marshes. In the end those who were organised into larger bands capitulated to the forces of the Caliph, but others dispersed into the wilderness of reeds and water and were heard of no more. Those who surrendered were described as pure barbarians, speaking no Arabic, and eating both carrion and human flesh.

It would be strange if so great a body of men had left no descendants in the marshlands.

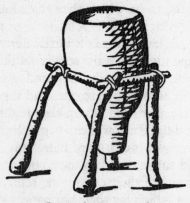

Porous-clay water vessel

Chapter Two

AFTER four days in Basra we left, unromantically, by taxi; the five of us huddled into one car with a mountain of luggage that was composed almost entirely of medicine chests.

Of that hour's journey, because it was succeeded by so much that was new to me, I have small recollection. A flat, dusty road that led at times through palm groves; a desert of still dry seasonal marsh; flat mud-coloured land under an open blue sky on which, endlessly, the black kites soared and swooped; by the roadside an eagle, heraldic and defiant, upon the carcase of a yellow pi-dog.

At length we left the road and began to drive away from it over hard, dry mud, cut by shallow irrigation ditches over which the taxi lurched perilously in the direction of a distant palm grove, and within a stone's throw of the Euphrates beyond was a village of date-cultivators to which Thesiger's crew had brought his canoe.

After the glare of light outside it seemed very dark under the palms, and our surroundings very unfamiliar. We were among the scattered reed houses of a village, the ground between them intersected by deep water-filled ditches, each spanned by a felled palm log, worn and slippery from the passage of many feet. Across these precarious bridges we threaded our way towards a reed building many times larger than any other in sight, the *mudhif*, or guest-house, of a sheikh.

These *mudhifs* are a feature of all the country surrounding the marshlands. They are used solely for the entertaining of guests, who may eat and sleep there—customarily for not more than one night—even though they be casual strangers. The *mudhifs* consist, as do other reed houses, of a row of arches made from the giant twenty-foot reed *Phragmites communis*, over which reed matting is laid to form a structure not unlike a nissen hut, but often of nobler proportions. The number of arches is always uneven, nine, eleven, thirteen or fifteen, and the entrance faces towards Mecca. This entrance is low at one of the two flat ends, and in the great majority of *mudhifs* it is also the only entrance for light, though some of the more ornate buildings have intricate and ornate reed lattice work at the opposite end. In either case the light is dim, and the atmosphere beneath the high smoke-darkened arches reminiscent of a cathedral. A *mudhif* customarily contains no furniture; when guests arrive servants spread rugs on the reed matting floor, and place bolster-shaped cushions of green or crimson plush along the walls. As everywhere else outside the towns the habitual seated position is cross-legged upon the floor. The coffee hearth, about a third of the way from the entrance, is a small strip where the mud floor is bare of covering, and beside it stands a row of brass and copper coffee pots of varying sizes. Among these is a King coffee pot with an ornamented symbol sprouting from the lid; these seem vessels of ritual significance in keeping with the solemnity of the building.

The sheikh himself was away, and we were greeted by his brother, a man of whom I chiefly remember his chin—or his absence of it, for he had less than any human being I have ever seen. A short fringe of grey beard marked the position it should have occupied; but for it a line drawn from his lower lip to his Adam's apple would have encountered no obstacle.

At this stage, the outset of our journey, I was entirely ignorant of the manners and customs that constitute good behaviour; the majority of these are common to a great part of the Arab world, and in no way peculiar to the marshlands, but most were new to me. Some I acquired by example, but in the most important Thesiger had instructed me before we left Basra. I knew the simplest forms of greeting, and that one should place one's hand over one's heart after shaking hands; that one should be barefoot when entering a house (but should be careful to wear shoes outside, for fear of hookworm); that the left hand is unclean and should be used only for unclean tasks.

This last is the most difficult for the inexperienced European to remember, for few realise the comparatively high degree of ambidexterity they have attained. While right-handed people do not use the left hand for the direct performance of any skilled task, it is constantly and unconsciously in use as an adjunct or supplement, and very soon I found that a conscious effort of will was required to keep it unoccupied.

We are, by Arab standards, a very insanitary people. The idea of using lavatory paper is disgusting to them; nothing can cleanse except water, or, in the case of the desert Arabs, sand. For this they use the left hand, and there is nothing perfunctory about the washing; a man will continue until he is satisfied, which may be several minutes. In theory—but not always, it must be admitted, in practice—a man will also wash himself after urinating, which is always done in a squatting position.

Because it is the left hand that performs these and other unclean tasks it becomes a thing unclean in itself; and is never, as is the right hand, ornamented with rings. It should not, however scrupulously it has been washed, touch the face or head, or be used to hold a cigarette; or be put to any one of the numberless and often aimless uses (such as meditative pinching of the lip or stroking of the chin) which pass unnoticed among Europeans.

The idea of cleanliness, however far practice may fall short of theory, is very strong among even primitive Arabs. That it is a shameful thing to allow pubic hair to grow, probably has its origin in the same idea. It is very rare to see dirty nails, either of hands or of feet, and immediately before eating, after the party is seated, a host or his servant will always carry round a small ewer and bowl for rinsing the fingers. It is customary, too, to rinse the mouth after eating.

Eating in the Arab manner requires to be learnt, and at the beginning I found it humiliatingly impossible. The *pièce de résistance* of all meals is the same, a conical mountain of rice which is often two feet across and a foot high, and its manipulation is not easily mastered. The guests sit cross-legged on the floor before one or more of these mountains, round which, in a sheikh's *mudhif*, are usually ranged bowls of gravy, mutton, whole small chickens, and plates of a thin greyish gelatinous substance tasting like the smell of scented soap. All this is to be eaten with the hand, and the right hand only, though the left may be used to hold a chicken while the right pulls the carcase apart. Any Arab host worthy of the name will kill chickens—worth about four shillings each—for his guests, and a hospitable sheikh will sometimes kill a sheep, whose boiled and nauseous head is placed among the other dishes to announce the fact. Pieces of flesh from the ears, the hair still attached, are esteemed as a delicacy, and hospitable fingers explore for a guest the gums and palate, producing strips and morsels which would be appetising if the head were not staring at the eater with those dreadful boiled eyes.

I have found in Desmond Stewart's *New Babylon* an Arab proverb which I did not know when I was in Iraq, and which would have explained a great deal to me if I had: "Eat like a camel and be the first to finish." Every meal is, indeed, a sort of eating race, and each man crams himself feverishly, in a silence unbroken but for champing jaws and an occasional belch. Whatever the embellishments, the rice is the main meal. One pours a little gravy over the claim one has staked on the mountain slope, and digs in a fist. This should be done with the back of the hand uppermost and the thumb on the palm; the fingers enclose the rice, and when the hand reaches the mouth the thumb pushes the rice up into it—if, that is to say, there is any rice left to push.

That first evening, I found, there rarely was. The mere fact of being cross-legged made the rice a disconcertingly long way off, and no matter how large a handful I set out with, so to speak, it had dwindled to a few grains by the time the hand reached the mouth. Such of the intervening space as was not occupied by my lap was covered by a section of the gigantic waterproof floor-cloth that the servants had spread before laying the meal; on to this resonant surface the rice from my hand pattered and plopped like a hail shower. I began to cheat wildly, pouring on more gravy and squeezing the rice into adhesive balls in my palm; for the first week this, though an acknowledgment of defeat, was the only method I found possible.

When the eating race was over—and Thesiger, who had introduced among his own men the Bedouin custom of rising simultaneously, was an easy winner—it became clear that, however efficient were the other contestants, there were many messy feeders among them, for on the great cloth lay several pounds of scattered rice among the bones and other discarded litter.

Eventually I became able to eat rice quickly and efficiently, without spilling a grain; but to the end, though I could detect no difference between my handling of it and theirs, the Arabs insisted that I was somehow doing it wrong.

When one has eaten, one's right hand is necessarily covered in rice and dripping oily gravy, and it is quite in order to clean the hand by licking it. If, however, a chicken has been part of the menu, the left hand, which has been allowed to hold while the right hand mauls, is equally covered with gravy and fragments; and to me it proved practically impossible to remember that if one is licking one food-covered hand one may not lick the other. After my first *gaucheries* of this kind my left hand seemed to be preternaturally large and ugly; I seemed to perceive all at once the grotesqueness of the human hand, even its pathos; those five defiantly mobile fingers that might work only hidden and in shame.

There were rules to be learnt, too, about the drinking of coffee, which, though few of the common people can afford it, any man of importance customarily offers to his guests. The beans are ground, by pestle and mortar, and then roasted over the fire; the *mores* require that both operations should be done in the presence of the guest, and no host would dream of offering previously prepared coffee. When it has been poured from pot to pot among the rank at the coffee hearth, in a sequence that I never properly understood, a servant approaches the seated guest carrying in one hand the coffee pot and in the other a doll-sized cup. Into the cup he pours about a dessertspoonful, and this the guest drinks— if he can, for it is almost boiling—at a gulp. If he wants no more he shakes the cup quickly as he returns it; it is, in any case, bad manners to drink more than three cups before giving this sign.

Though belching is entirely socially acceptable, there is the strongest possible taboo against breaking wind; it is among the deadliest of all social sins. Most of the Arabs have done so at one time or another during their lives, but it is so memorable an event that by it other more momentous happenings are dated; it remains evergreen in their memories. When asked for the date of a murder or a family disaster a man may muse and then reply, "I don't know; I think it was the year that Jassim farted."

In illustration of this there is a story much like another of Elizabethan England, and which has, no doubt, many parallels in other cultures holding the same taboos.

Abarachdan was a youth, the son of a sheikh, who had recently been admitted to the *medres*, or council of sheikhs, at

Baghdad. There, in public he committed the unpardonable crime. It echoed through the *medres*, it echoed through all Baghdad. He was driven from the *medres* by his outraged elders, hounded out of Baghdad, and finally from all Iraq. He spent his life in Egypt, and when he was an old man he returned to spend the last years of his life in the country of his birth. He came back on foot, frail and weary. Before he reached the frontier of Iraq, while he was still in Syria, he paused to rest and drink at a well. There he saw a boy drawing water, and fell into conversation with him. After a time Abarachdan asked the boy his age. "I do not know," the child replied (for few Arabs know the year of their birth), "but I know that my father was born in the year that one Abarachdan farted in the *medres* in Baghdad."

Abarachdan returned sorrowing into exile, for his lifetime had not been enough to expiate his crime.

In one of the narrow scum-covered ditches that threaded the village lay Thesiger's canoe, left here by Amara, Sabeti, and Hassan before they had come out to meet us in Basra. Canoe is a mean word for so beautiful a craft. The canoes of Southern Iraq are of many shapes and sizes, often squat and primitive-looking, but this was a *tarada*, or war canoe, thirty-six feet long and less than three and a half feet at its widest beam, with a high slender prow rising five feet from the water in a curve like an eagle's claw. This is the aristocrat of all craft of the marshes, ornamented throughout the interior with round iron bosses like those of a medieval castle door. The high prow enables them to force their way through reed beds where a conventionally shaped boat would stick, and their shallow draught of a few inches gives them free passage over water no more than ankle deep.

Few men other than sheikhs own a *tarada*, for whereas canoes of other types may cost as little as £3 or £4, a *tarada* costs £75, and its possession, among people who are in the main poor, is a hall-mark of status, as certain makes of car used once to be in England.

At dusk we walked through the palm grove, past the waiting *tarada* and down to the bank of the Euphrates. There were no craft upon the river, and beyond it the horizon was flat and bare; on the ultimate distance lay a dim darker strip, the great reeds of the permanent marsh.

When we lay down to sleep in the *mudhif* that night it was of the marshes that I dreamt. All through the darkness the dogs of the village barked and growled, and by the fire at the coffee hearth sat three armed negroes whose faces coloured my dreams, dreams of reeds as tall as forest trees between whose stems skulked the centuries-dead cannibal army of the Zenj. Between dreams I remember the low chatter of the negroes' voices, and I remember fleas, fleas, fleas. In the dawn there came a rustle of rain on the reed roof, and the far-away crying of wild geese.

In the morning, grey and cold as an English autumn, the fourth member of Thesiger's crew arrived. Kathia was one of those confusing people of whom one's first impression is almost necessarily misleading, whose personalities seem after a little while to disintegrate into seemingly unrelated facets. He was a big chunky youth of nineteen or twenty, with perceptibly Mongolian features. There are a number of this type in the marshes, possibly remote descendants of the pillaging armies of Hulagu, grandson of Jengis Khan, who at his sack of Baghdad in 1285 slaughtered nearly a million peaceful citizens. (He deliberated for a while whether or not to kill their ruler, the Caliph, and brought together a meeting of clairvoyants to tell him whether some cataclysm of nature would result from this act. The seers replied cautiously that none had followed the martyrdoms of John the Baptist, Jesus Christ, or Hussain; so Hulagu took a risk on it, and put the Caliph to death in circumstances of peculiar horror.)

Kathia, who seemed at first sight happy, extravert, and competent, was in fact a neurotic, subject to alternating moods of depression and gaiety, and was by far the least reliable of the four.

We loaded the *tarada*, and as the crew manœuvred its great length through the ditches of the palm village, lifting the palm-trunk bridges as bridges over great waterways are lifted to give passage to large vessels, the true journey began.

We turned out into the Euphrates and followed its near bank upstream for a mile or so before crossing to Huwair on the north bank. Huwair is a busy, teeming village of reed houses, one of the boat-building centres on which the marshmen and riverside dwellers are dependent. Because there is no wood in the marshes, and little in all Southern Iraq but palm trees, the materials are all imported except the bitumen with which all canoes are coated.

This boat-building community contained a very high proportion of Sayids (those claiming descent from the Prophet), who become rarer the farther one penetrates into the permanent marshlands. Sayids distinguish themselves in dress by the wearing of a dark blue headcloth, which is usually the normal Shi'a black-and-white *keffia* with the addition of dye. Some of these men are wanderers, more or less parasitic upon the peoples with whom they live temporarily, for they claim the right of support by virtue of their holy descent; others, on the waterways that surround the marshes, live in communities where they preponderate, and are as industrious as other men.

It is the Sayids who are most inclined to be hostile to the Christian, or to anyone who is not of the faith, and Thesiger had, early in his exploration of the area, found difficulties to be overcome. One Sayid, a fellow guest at a house where Thesiger already had friends, publicly rebuked his host for the presence of an unbeliever, and lamented the decay of the faith which allowed unclean Christians to eat in the houses of the faithful. It was probably the publicity of this attack that tipped the scales in Thesiger's favour, for no Arab host could permit his guest to be slighted or insulted. He replied to the Sayid that he was no theologian, but that Thesiger was his guest and should be treated as such; and as for cleanliness he seemed at least quite as clean as they were. After this forthright statement of policy the other guests in the house felt required to declare their sympathies, and one by one they left the side of the Sayid and came to sit with Thesiger. A little later he was able, in several villages, to doctor Sayids' children and was by now accepted by the majority. At Huwair, however, I noticed that they would not drink from the same vessels as we did; they washed the cups immediately after we had used them, and with what seemed an unnecessary ostentation.

We stayed at Huwair only long enough to have new paddles made for the *tarada*, and in the afternoon we left for Ramla, the last of the dry land villages before the great marsh.

Sheepskin butter churn

Chapter Three

IT was blowing hard and cold when we left the village, and the sky was empty and grey without individual clouds. We left the palm groves and the stretches of dry land behind us, and soon the horizon was flat and bare, and the yard high stubble of burnt reeds and bulrushes through which the ill-defined watercourses ran was paler than the blue-grey horizon sky. Very far away in front of us a few dark specks showed the last of the palm groves before the edge of the permanent marsh. The earth seemed flat as a plate and stretched away for ever before us, vast, desolate and pallid; pale bulrush stubble standing in water that reflected a vast pale sky, against which strained here and there the delicate shape of a long reed bent before the wind, the silhouette urgent as the keening of a violin. As the gusts grew stronger and ruffled the water among the reeds into flurries of small ripples, it tore a chorus of strange sounds from the stiff, withered sedge stumps, groans and whistles, bleats and croaks, and loud crude sounds of flatulence; if the devils of Hieronymus Bosch could speak from the canvas this would be the babel of their tongues, these the derisive notes of the trumpets at their backsides.

There was no colour anywhere, and the grey sky, unbroken by hill or tree, seemed as immense as from a small boat far out at sea. Occasionally a flight of pelicans would sail majestically by, riding the wind on stiff outstretched wings, rigid and bulky in body as seaplanes; and once a flock of white ibis drifted past very high up, to fan out into a wheeling kaleidoscope of white petals on the great empty sky. It was in some way a terrible landscape, utterly without human sympathy, more desolate and inimical than the sea itself, except, perhaps, when it breaks in winter on a long shingle beach and the land behind it is flat. Here in the limit-less stubble of pale bulrush one felt that no sheltering ship could sail nor human foot walk, and there seemed no refuge for any creature whose blood was warm.

For three hours after, we moved through this unchanging landscape with the weird clamour of the reeds about us, while the little dark blot of the palm grove at Ramla grew slowly bigger, and at length we were in waterways where the reed stubble grew on firm ground at our sides, and the reed houses of Ramla showed huddled round the palms.

Though Ramla stood on a low mud island with scattered palm groves about it, and thus was not a true Ma'dan village, it was yet the first of the primitive communities I had seen, for at Huwair we had been close to the road and to civilisation, and had stayed in the *mudhif* of a sheikh and not with the common people. Here the houses were small, some twelve feet wide by thirty-five feet long, and many of them appeared disordered by the gale that tossed and flung the threshing palm trees into alternately beckoning and sup-pliant shapes. The shallow water of the marsh petered out into mudbanked ditches and scum-covered backwaters among the houses, and above the level of the water the wind churned up an eddying dust-storm of sand and small reed fragments. A group waited for us on a bank by one of the nearer houses, their robes and headcloths flapping wildly, and after the first exchange of greetings we were ushered—as I was to regret so often and for so many reasons in so many other villages—straight into the house. The entrance was a slit in the vertical reeds forming the end of the house, so narrow that one could only enter sideways.

At this early stage in the journey I was as nervous of committing social *gaffes* as a worshipper in a church with whose ritual he is not familiar. I had been careful to put my hand over my heart after shaking hands, as did those who greeted me, and had been at a loss for response when one of them kissed my hand; now, as I was halfway through the door, I remembered that I should be barefoot in the house. My shoe lace ran into a knot, and the party fretted behind me while I unravelled it half in and half out of the entrance.

Inside, the house was like the vast majority of all those in the marshes. There were nine reed arches, and halfway along a low bed-like platform, also made entirely of reeds, jutted out from the right-hand wall and divided the house, by effect rather than by fact, in two roughly equal halves. The platform is in fact not a bed, despite its resemblance to one, for the marshmen always sleep on the floor. It is used as a European would use a cupboard, for storage of household goods, and on this one were stacked canoe paddles, grain, blankets, pillows, and other things that were indistinct in the darkness, for no reed house ever has a window.

The two halves of the house correspond roughly to the two ground-floor rooms of an old-fashioned cottage; one is the cottage kitchen, in which the family cooks, eats, sits, and in this case sleeps, and the other is the "parlour", which is rarely used except for guests. Beyond the platform I could see women and children squatting round a fire and a cooking pot on a tripod, and the light from the flames shone also upon various livestock, two dogs, a cat, a number of chickens, and three calves. On the near side of the platform the floor was laid with the same reed matting as covered the outside of the house, four strips of it laid to leave a bare patch in the centre where a small fire of reeds burned beside a row of coffee pots. Our host fetched cushions with hard wool covers woven in bright designs, and in a moment we were seated cross-legged again as we had been in the *tarada*. This, though I did not yet know it, was to be the pattern of the whole journey; two or three hours of sitting cross-legged is painful to those unaccustomed to it, and to step out of the canoe only to resume the same position in a matter of seconds can be real torture.

We drank dessertspoonfuls of coffee from tiny cups as we

had done at Huwair, and then we drank tea from minute glasses half filled with sugar, which is what every marshman offers to his guests, even when he cannot afford coffee. As the hours passed, the house began to fill up, until at last there were more than sixty people crowded on to the floor of that eighteen-by-twelve-foot space; all men and boys, for the women are kept apart, and may not mingle with menfolk outside their own families. It would seem impossible for that sardine-pack to be in any order of precedence, yet they were; and each, too, somehow avoided presenting a complete back view to the man behind him, for that, like presenting the sole of an outstretched foot, is the height of bad manners.

I was astonished by the rigmarole of social ritual with which these primitive people surrounded themselves. Each entering guest greeted his host, and in some cases the formal exchange of greetings between the two was extended to a machine-gun fire of fifteen or twenty questions and answers. Then the guest would select a place and sit down, but the social duties of his arrival had only just begun. No sooner had he settled himself cross-legged in his cramped position than a single voice out of the crowd would bid him good evening.

"Messàkum Allâh bil khair."

The newcomer would half rise to his feet, his legs still scissored under him.

"Messàkum Allâh bil khair, Ahmed," he responded, and began to settle himself again. Then it came from another corner of the room, and again he would bob up on the triangle of his crossed ankles. "Messàkum Allâh bil khair, Daoud," and soon he would be bouncing up and down like a piston. "Messàkum Allâh bil khair, Mahommed," "Messàkum Allâh bil khair, Hussein," "Messàkum Allâh bil khair, Faleh," until every grown man in the room had shot his round and the newcomer could relax and time the firing of his own ammunition at the next comer.

Presently a lantern was lit and stood on the dividing platform at the centre of the house, but its little circle of illumination was closed in by the figures round it, and the throng of faces was lit only by the wildly flickering fire of reeds. Our host knelt at the hearth with a great bundle of reeds gripped between his knees, and as the fire consumed them with big wind-gusted flames he moved the bundle up a foot at a time. The fire was like the end of a moving staircase, where the conveyor slides out of sight under the firm ground. Each time as he thrust the reeds farther up into the flames a frantic exodus of small dun-coloured caterpillars could be seen hurrying along the stems away from the fire, going the wrong way on the moving staircase; but the reeds burned slower than the caterpillars could hunch along, so that they always won in the end. I lost sight of them between our host's knees, and as they seemed never to reappear I wondered what became of them.

It was beyond my understanding that the house did not catch fire. The gale roared and rattled in the reed matting outside; the burning reeds crackled and flared and the sparks flew upward and glowed in the dim reed roof; cigarettes were stubbed out vaguely and at random on the dry reed matting of the floor. It seemed as though either the reed house or the flames and the sparks must be an illusion, a montage for a cinema set, or a superimposition. I wondered what premium a European insurance company would set on a policy to cover these houses against fire.

In fact the gale that night did start a fire in a neighbouring village, and left half its inhabitants homeless; one of the greatest disasters, other than death or disease, that can afflict the marsh people; for they may have to travel great distances to replace the high reeds from which the houses are built, and to buy at the time of their greatest poverty the new reed matting with which to cover them.

This was my first night in a village house, and but for one incident it was typical enough of the pattern of all those that followed it. Sometime before midnight Thesiger said that we were ready to sleep, and the assembled company of guests began to file out of the house. Our host scattered the ashes of the fire, and our canoe boys spread out blankets on the floor about it and disposed our effects with the extreme precaution against robbery that is customary in the marshes. Jacket and trousers formed the pillow, and Sabeti, who had assumed responsibility for me, stowed my every possession beneath my sleeping bag—field-glasses, camera, gun—until I felt like a Gulliver reclining on a Lilliput mountain range. Then began the massage that is one of the strangest, and at times most painful, customs of marsh society. It is a deep kneading massage that seems to leave no muscle unexplored, and to the uninitiated it is at first extremely uncomfortable. The people themselves have the profoundest belief in its therapeutic value, but its practice is a purely social custom, a gesture of goodwill and friendship that may be extended to convey various shades of meaning. While it is practically a ritual before retiring, it may be employed at any time or in any place, and one's immediate neighbour as one sits among a crowd of guests in a house or stands in a throng out of doors may start work upon biceps or thigh as casually and thoughtlessly as he would play with the string of beads that is his inseparable toy.

Sabeti's massage was agonising on the limbs and ticklish on the torso; I squirmed under it for a quarter of an hour before I felt that good manners would permit me to say that it was enough. Thesiger, I noticed, was submitting to the combined mauling of Amara and Hassan with the greatest apparent equanimity. At last it was over, and the lantern was extinguished, and under the cover of the darkness I surreptitiously removed my gun and field-glasses from their excruciating position below my spine. The gun I laid in the few inches between me and the wall; I was barricaded in by the sleeping bodies of Sabeti, Hassan and Kathia, and to me it seemed secure enough from any thief in the night. I twined the strap of my field-glasses through the fingers of my left hand and went to sleep.

I sleep very lightly, and I woke with a start without knowing what had awoken me. It was quite dark, and there were gentle snores all round me, and not so gentle snores from Sabeti, whose shaven head was touching mine, as he shared my pillow with his feet in the opposite direction. I could see nothing at all but the paler slit of night sky at the door, and I could hear nothing else but the rattle and batter of the gale in the reeds of the house. I was about to settle down again when I felt a gentle exploratory tug on the strap of the field-glasses between my fingers. I moved my right hand over to the strap, and felt gently up it. I touched a hand, and instinctively I grabbed it; then, even as I did so, I realised that the fellow to it might be holding a knife, and as the fingers wrenched back out of mine I let go. For an instant the paler slit of the door was darkened as the visitor slipped out. I put my hand out in the dark and felt for my gun where I had laid it a few inches from my side and there was nothing there. I realised that my sybaritic attitude towards sleeping with a gun under my spine would be exposed, and my subterfuge revealed, but I felt that there was nothing for it but to wake Sabeti. I fished out a torch, confirmed that the gun was not there and did so. I could not explain to him what had happened, for my Arabic vocabulary was at that time limited to some dozen words, but I was able to say that the gun wasn't there. Sabeti launched on a low chatter of reproof that was as plain in sense as if he had spoken in English, and ended by throwing back his own blanket to show his legs scissored round my gun as though he were climbing a rope. I felt as foolish as he intended.

Our waking, too, was like many that followed it during the next two months. First, when one was still heavy with sleep, the insistent barking of dogs, outside but only a few feet from one's head, would invade unconsciousness, then the sounds of the household busying themselves beyond the dividing reed platform with preparations for the day. One could ignore the sound of the dogs, I found, but the sound of articulate human speech, even if the words were not understood, would not allow sleep. There would be the curiously defined and intimate ringing sound of a metal mortar pounding roasted coffee beans in a metal pestle, and on the floor near at hand the protesting groans and stretching of our awakening canoe boys. This would usually be punctuated with dull thuds, as Thesiger, with scout-masterish jocularity, belaboured their heads with a small pillow, hard and heavy-seeming as a sandbag; a treatment that he affected to believe painless. Washing was of ritual simplicity, a splash of cold water poured on one's hands from the unvarying long-spouted copper water jug as one squatted outside the door; we shaved every three or four days or when we were to be the guests of some sheikh. Blankets were folded and stowed and the fire lit at the coffee hearth in the middle of the floor, and we sat cross-legged round it to drink the tiny glasses of sweet tea and eat the thin bread that more prosperous households produce for their guests' breakfast. All Arab bread is unrecognisable by the European connotation of the word; for it is without yeast, greyish and pliable sheets of dough whose surface the flame of a mud oven has irregularly blackened. In the marshes the normal everyday bread, some half an inch thick is made by plastering the sheet of dough to the walls of an acorn-shaped mud oven, open at the top and with the fire burning in the middle of it, so that the flame licks the dough. The thin bread, however, which is something of a luxury and a dainty, is made by pouring a cream-like mixture of flour and water on to a large inverted smooth-bottomed plate supported on three clay bricks over the fire. A second plate, like the lid of a large saucepan, is placed over the bread, which can be peeled off after about a minute, golden coloured and very like a large pancake. Unlike the normal bread, which would be considered inedible by most Europeans, the thin bread is appetising both in appearance and in taste.

Immediately after breakfast Thesiger's surgery began, and since the gale was still roaring out of an empty blue sky outside, tearing up dust-storms from the dry mud of the island and filling the whole air with fluttering golden fragments of reed, it took place in the house. My admiration for Thesiger's assurance grew with every moment; there was surely no practitioner in England who would have attempted to treat the variety of complaints with which he was confronted. He had won his reputation among the marsh people by years of this work; rapid hit or miss diagnosis that grew gradually more accurate with prolonged experience, followed by the profligate use of the latest costly anti-biotic drugs that rendered the diagnosis of secondary importance.

The marshmen are riddled with diseases, many of them appalling to look at, and it is probably to their high mortality that they owe their continued existence, for this watery waste could never have supported an expanding population. Many of these diseases are acutely infectious, and when I left the marshes I left marvelling that I had contracted none, but marvelling much more that Thesiger had survived four years of intimate contact.

Dysentery is one of many diseases that are endemic; and in a marsh village, where the water comes right to the walls of the houses on every side, that drawn for drinking often contains recognisable fragments of human excrement besides a multiplicity of animal organisms so dense as to give the whole the appearance of a thick greenish soup. Yaws, a non-venereal relation of syphilis producing skin conditions of peculiar horror and high contagion, afflicts a great part of the population; ringworm or some allied skin affection may be expected in the heads of the greater number of children; hookworm spreads rapidly through the barefoot habit; and bilharzia is inescapable to the marshmen, who of necessity spend much of their time naked in the water. It is this last, perhaps, that might properly be described as the disease *par excellence* of the marshes, for no cure can prevent immediate reinfection. The bilharzia of the marshes is the parasite whose true name is *Schistosoma haematobium*, an organism about a centimetre long and a millimetre broad which ravages the pelvic region of its human hosts. In common with many other internal parasites it has an intermediate host, in this case the water snail, without whose total destruction the disease cannot be eliminated. At the stage of emergence from the snail the parasites are active burrowing organisms which penetrate the skin of a man and begin the next stage of their existence. An enormous number reach no fertile ground, as it were, and die, leaving wheals and blotches where they do so, but the operation partakes of the stupendous profligacy of all generation; and, teeming like spermatozoa, a number pass through the lung capillaries to the heart and are thence distributed all over the body. The first symptom is the passing of blood in the urine, and this continues until at its height some thirty thousand eggs are being passed every day. These, in the marshes, return to the water, where they at once hatch into another active embryo stage which enters the water snail. It follows that the stagnant water surrounding a marsh village is densely teeming with the organisms of the post-snail stage, and it is impossible for any member of the community to avoid infection.

The disease is very slow in progress, and one may play host to breeding bilharzia for years without more than mild discomfort if the infection is slight, but sooner or later all the pelvic organs may become affected and suffer severe pain and malfunction, besides secondary effects such as stones that form round the eggs in the bladder.

That list is but a tiny fraction of the diseases to which the marshmen are subject, and it is small wonder that Thesiger, who for four years had performed seeming miracles among them, was besieged by an importunate multitude in every village that we visited. The number of patients would grow gradually from a nucleus of two or three in the household with which we were staying; word would go round that the medicine chest was open, and they would come in from every quarter of the village to press round him, sometimes in hundreds. To treat them all would have been impossible; no medicine chest that could be transported in a *tarada* would have lasted more than two or three villages; and many, especially milder cases or those whom Thesiger suspected of malingering in order to be in the swim, were turned away. From the first day these decided that I was a suitable intermediary; of less formidable aspect, perhaps, than Thesiger, and one whose heart could be softened to plead for them. I was soon surrounded with a crowd little less than that which milled round him, and no amount of repetition that I did not understand Arabic made any noticeable impression upon either their numbers or verbosity. Each displayed his suffering with a formal and unvarying ritual of pathos; my view became a kaleidoscope of cataracted eyes, suppurating boil-craters, patches of angry rash on brown skins, wounds, and swollen genitals.

For nearly three hours Thesiger worked indefatigably in the midst of this bedlam; his hypodermic stabbed with piston-like regularity at brown bottoms; oceans of ointment were spread on leagues of lint; he stitched away like a tailor at dog bites and pig-gores, and counted out hundreds of white pills into hundreds of horny brown hands; while all space and light were effectively closed off by waiting patients and relations.

Last of all came the circumcisions. During Thesiger's first year among these people he had been in much demand to repair the often spectacular damage inflicted by wandering professional circumcisers, who, in return for a fee of five shillings, would perform a protracted and agonising mutilation whose aftermath of sepsis and slow convalescence lasted often for many months. The near-universality of sepsis and complication had at first puzzled Thesiger, for by the very nature of their lives the marshmen have built up some small immunity, and it was not for some time that he discovered the almost incredible cause. The wandering circumcisers, to give full measure for their five-shilling fee, were in the habit of dressing the wound with a magic powder of which they carried considerable quantities; and this powder, it turned out, was composed entirely of dried and powdered foreskins. Thesiger's despairing attempt to explain the rudimentary principles of anti-sepsis had brought furious scowls from the purveyors of the powder, and pleas from the suffering people that he would perform the operation himself. His first attempts had proved so rapid, painless, and free from after-effect that his competitors had felt inspired to put about a rumour that he rendered his patients sterile. Thesiger was so constantly on the move that they could not be aware of the weakness in this otherwise intelligent gambit, for they did not know how many grown boys and young men had been among his patients. By the following year a large number of them had fathered healthy babies, and the wandering circumcisers found themselves discredited as liars as well as butchers. Thesiger had taken the terror from the operation, and now few would consent to have it performed by anyone else. Would-be patients who had heard of our vicinity would sometimes follow us for many days, and would come in from neighbouring villages to wherever we were known to be staying.

Circumcision, which is normally performed in an arbitrarily chosen year somewhere between the ages of ten and nineteen, is something of an occasion, though the extreme informality of the proceedings is in contrast with that of many other peoples who perform ritual mutilations. The boys assemble, anything from one or two to fifty or more, and lie upon the ground in rows while the operator

42

moves round them as a doctor might move from bed to bed in a hospital ward. The greater part of the whole village forms a solid wall of spectators; women and girls of all ages form an appreciable part of the audience; and often a boy's mother or sister will sit beside him, encouraging him before the operation and keeping the flies off him after it. Only occasionally a boy professes embarrassment at the presence of the women, and asks to be operated upon in surreptitious privacy; the true marshmen are so often naked in the presence of women that no element of shame attaches to it. Little sympathy, and often much mockery, is shown to a boy who is frightened or who cries out, but very few do, and I have heard one who was asked what Thesiger's operation felt like reply "it felt as if a flea bit me". As the operation is completed the boy's mother gives vent to the weird cry of rejoicing that is described in technical literature as "ululating" (an onomatopœic word, for the sound is simply "ulululululululululu" repeated in a high and rapid wail until breath gives out), and sometimes the father fires a shot or two from a rifle. Often each boy of a group that is circumcised together gives a small feast for the others, and it is said that some sort of bond or blood brothership grows amongst them.

After the circumcision the boys remain recumbent for an hour, as a safeguard against bleeding, and then they walk home. From then on, during the few days until they are healed, they wear two or three onions on a string round their necks, for the people are convinced that the wound will become septic if the boy should smell cooking, or baking, or any form of perfume. The boy who is in the vicinity of such smells will plug his nostrils with the small ends of the onions until the danger is past. Curiously, they believe the peril to emanate from these pleasant scents, never from stenches; furthermore native custom had previously required the operation to be performed in the height of summer, as the operators had held that cool weather would cause the wound to become inflamed.

The gale blew unabated all afternoon, and by now it was clear that we must spend a second night at Ramla. As a rule Thesiger was at pains not to spend two nights under the same roof, for in the eyes of most marsh Arabs the demands of hospitality include the killing of chickens, and become a serious drain upon the householder's resources.

I should have liked to wander over the small stretches of dry ground surrounding the village, but because of the dogs it was impossible; this too was a repetitive pattern throughout the long journey. Practically every house in the marshes is guarded by at least one, and sometimes as many as four or five large and almost invariably savage dogs. They are savage both because they are trained to be so and because, being an unclean animal, they are afforded little of the casual affection that household watch-dogs may receive outside the Muslim world. Their attitude to all human beings other than those of the household they guard is dour, morose, and explosive. They bark so incessantly both by day and by night that many of them have strained their vocal chords; some produce no more than a husky whisper, others the cracked and disconcertingly alternating bellow and squeak of the human adolescent. As a result of constant and venomous bickering among themselves the older dogs are so tattered and frayed as to give the impression of being damaged beyond all reasonable hope of repair; their ears, if they still possess them, serrated like the fronds of a fern, their tails lopped to haphazard half-lengths, even the black buttons of their noses sometimes twisted to preposterous angles with their faces, or hanging by a thread of gristle; their flanks and shoulders criss-crossed with the scars of teeth. The basic type, before this distortion has been superimposed, is something between an Alsatian

44

and a Husky, with a dense, usually light coloured, coat, and a tail that curls more or less tightly upward. The commonest pattern is sand-coloured or rufous, and suggests descent from the wild red dogs of India, but they may be blotched or brindled, and occasionally white. Whatever their origin they must by now have reached the maximum development of which the species is capable; there are no small dogs and no unaggressive dogs, quite simply because if there were they would be killed by the large and aggressive.

The religious—or in this case customary, for the marsh-men cannot be said to possess more than the *mores* of their nominal religion—uncleanness of dogs does not prevent them being on terms of some familiarity with the household they serve, and more especially its younger members. The adults discourage a display of affection, but despite these sanctions I have seen children sleeping with puppies cuddled in their arms, and occasionally older children will play with a dog as do Europeans. Even in their unsenti-mental society the protection between dog and man is to a large extent mutual, and the killing of a dog can start a blood-feud as does the killing of a human being.

The dogs effectively restrict a stranger's movements in a village or about its immediate precincts, and because of them it is impossible even to relieve oneself without a guard standing by; indeed it is surprising that the marshmen man-age somehow to steal from each other as much as they do.

At nightfall the wind was still gusty and tumultuous, but its force must have slackened a little, for an exhausted fish-ing party made its way into the village after three days marooned without food on a small island. They had been poisoning fish, the only mass method of fishing that the marshmen allow themselves. For some forgotten reason fishing with nets is taboo, and the people who make their living in this way, the *Berbera*, are looked down upon as of low caste, so that the marsh tribesmen themselves are confined either to the grotesquely inefficient methods of spearing or of strewing the water with poisoned bait; digitalis concealed in shrimps. The poisoned fish float to the surface, and their poaching by passing boats gives rise to frequent squabbles.

Night came down upon the marshes in utter desolation; there was no sunset nor hint of colour, the light just faded out of that roaring grey sky until the silhouettes of the tossing palm plumes became dim and indistinct and merged into the darkness of a starless sky. The house began to fill with guests as before, and when we had eaten and become once more part of a huddled throng who faced inward to the rearing flames of the reed fire, our host turned to a young man near him and asked him to sing. "Ma'agdar, Ma'agdar, I can't, I can't," he replied with the preliminary and quite meaningless modesty that I found to be customary, but after a few moments of protestation in diminuendo he composed himself and began. It was a quartet; he sang the melody, while three companions held an even chord like the drones of a bagpipe; like bagpipe music, too, it was at first difficult for an uneducated ear to discover any defined melody. The voice was tenor, and as with many other primitive peoples it was produced nasally and with a constant tremolo, whose range seemed at times greater than that of the melody itself. At first I found it too curious and unfamiliar to be acceptable, but as song succeeded song I became engulfed by it and permeated with it and its poignancy began to move me; even the absorption and strain with which the strangely unvocal notes were produced enhanced rather than detracted from the total effect. Most of the marshmen are quite unable to sing and know it, but the knowledge in no way deters them from trying; daylong, for example, Hassan as he paddled our canoe would from his position a yard astern of me pour forth his profuse and noticeably unpremeditated strains, a cracked and

46

excruciating nasal shout whose impact on the ear drum was not unlike that of a crackling telephone. The approved method of voice production makes enormous demands upon the singer, and when he has failed to master it the result is no less than disastrous. In almost every village, however, there are a few whose voices, perhaps because of their purity in childhood, have had continuous enough practice to become accomplished; their singing can be both beautiful and evocative, and they are in great demand for the entertaining of guests or for any other occasion of feasting.

When the singing was over our host called to a young negro slave with a humorous and *sympathique* face and asked him to dance. "Ma'agdar, Ma'agdar," he protested, as the singer had, but soon he was on his feet, and the squatting crowd shuffled a foot or two back from the fire, leaving him a space perhaps five feet by five.

I realised in the first few seconds that though the marsh-men's singing required a co-operative effort from the listener a little akin to that demanded of a hypnotic subject, the impact of the dancing was full and complete and to me irresistible. The rhythm was staccato yet somehow fluid, each movement whether of limb or torso somehow resembling a pause and a pounce. The dance was a narrative, as are many of them, and song and mime was a part of it, all held within the framework of a tight unvarying iambic rhythm. *Ti-tumti-túm, ti-tumti-túm*; the audience took up the rhythm, each stamping out the tune with the heel of an extended right foot, each with his arms outstretched before him and his hands locked with extended fingers to produce a finger-click as loud, literally, as a man may make by clapping his palms together. Even the small children can do this; a shrimp of six years can with his soft baby fingers make a crack like the report of a small pistol.

I could not follow the words that the slave sang as he danced, but the mime made the theme plain, a labourer cheated of his hire. His voice was light and plaintive and whimsically protesting; its pathos seemed the aggregate of generations of unquestioning slave tradition. As the dance neared its end he squatted on his heels and in exaggerated time with the rhythm he bounced round the little open space, searching for the labourer's hire of which he had been cheated, lifting the corners of the reed matting, peering into the coffee pots and among the embers of the fire, chanting pitifully, "I want my pay, I want my pay."

The next dance was, like most that I saw during the journey, erotic. These dances have been described in the journals of learned societies as "erotic but not obscene"; the distinction is a nice one, but the words would require close definition before the point could be maintained. Most of the movements in these dances are specifically and frankly sexual; sometimes the dance is composed almost exclusively of such movements, and becomes a stylised pantomime of the sexual act, ending with a formula to represent climax; sometimes the sexual movements are used arbitrarily among others, as though a dancer were using his whole repertoire and adding these for piquancy. Each dancer is in any case his own choreographer; he learns gradually when he is very small how to perform and perfect simple steps and body movements, and these he develops, elaborates, and intermingles into dances that are thus essentially his own though using the dance-language of his culture.

It seems likely that many hundreds of generations of dancing in the tiny confined space about the hearth of reed huts, with the necessity for the maximum movement in the minimum space, have been responsible for the great development of body-movement as opposed to footwork for which there would be inadequate room. Thus, any dancer worthy of the claim, often if he is still quite a small child, is able to call into play groups of muscles of whose very existence in himself the average European is unaware; and an important part of every dancer's vocabulary, as it were, is a violent and prolonged shivering of one or both shoulders. Precise and almost acrobatic use of the pelvic muscles lends a sexual flavour to nearly all dancing, the movements ranging from direct crissation to sinuous rolling motions or plain high-speed bottom waggling; this last nearly always draws enthusiastic laughter from the audience.

The slave's second dance that night at Ramla was on a theme that is very familiar to the marshmen, an exploitation of the *risqué* possibilities inherent in the Muslim attitude of prayer with the forehead pressed to the ground and the rump high in the air. He was a superb artist, and there was certainly nothing slipshod or haphazard in the execution of the performance, but whether it would have been labelled erotic rather than obscene in England seems a very academic point; it was a beautifully danced dirty joke.

Besides the talented and enthusiastic amateurs, of whom there are a number in every village, there are also professional dancers, or rather entertainers, for they are expected also to sing, to drum, and to perform "variety turns". They travel among the villages, and they are, of course, all male, for no woman ever makes an officially public appearance. The boys wear their hair long, and the rhythmic swinging of its heavy dark mass is a feature of their dancing; a thing that I never saw, for the only professional dancing boy we met with other than in the streets of Basra had had his hair shorn two days before, in preparation for school. In view of the erotic nature of the dancing itself it is perhaps not surprising that these boys are also semi-professional prostitutes, but they marry young, and often bring up their own children in the same tradition.

Among the villagers themselves, children are encouraged to dance from their earliest years, and at no age does absorption with or great skill in dancing carry any un-masculine connotations. A very good dancer, whether child or adult, is generally very good at everything else, and must, too, possess enormous physical energy, for the dances are long, violent and exhausting, and the audience calls for repeated encores. They are intolerant of a bad adult performer, but I have seen some sixty or seventy men and boys maintain a feigned absorption for half an hour while a five year old flopped and stumbled his unconvincing way through an interminable impromptu.

It was long after midnight when the singing and dancing were over and we finally settled down to sleep. The gale still roared outside and rustled and rattled the house of reeds and probed under the reed matting on the floor, lifting it in undulating waves like a ground swell at sea. Both Thesiger and I were impatient to leave Ramla, he because of the burden that he placed upon our host, and I because the true marshes were still before us and I felt that we were lingering on the threshold.

Marshmen's daggers

Chapter Four

IN the morning the clouds had gone, but the wind still blew like an express train. Thesiger was not at ease about our departure.

"We've got to go, and that's all there is to it. This man's killed half his chickens already, and it may blow like this for days. Trouble is to get where we're going we have to cross Zikri, which is a lake of more or less open water a dozen miles across. People get drowned there every year, and the boys are scared; the *tarada* won't stand much in the way of waves with all this baggage on board."

We left at about nine-thirty, and my last sight of the dry land was the mad semaphore of the palm branches and the billowing, fluttering clothing of the group who stood below them to wave us good-bye. Our host of the past two nights accompanied us as a pilot, paddling a little flat hunting canoe that had little more than two inches freeboard and looked as if the first gust of wind must swamp it.

The defined waterways grew fewer and disappeared, and soon we were amid a maze of crooked alleys in a jungle of trumpeting wind-tormented reed stumps and withered sedge. Gradually the channels grew wider and less distinguishable, until we were moving through open blue lagoons fringed and islanded with giant golden reeds growing dense and twenty feet high. They were as ripe standing corn must appear to a mouse, huge and golden in the sun, with only a tiny fringe of new green growth in the blue water at their feet. As yet there were so many islands that it was easy to find shelter; they were dense and solid-seeming and only their very tops bent under the gale that urged them majestically over the water, for most of these islands are unanchored, and drift slowly about the lagoons as calved icebergs drift in polar seas. Between them one could glimpse the open water of the lake itself, ruffled and royal blue under the sun, stretching away to where, very far off, the confining reed-beds at the farther side looked like long yellow cliffs of sand. There were no definable edges to the lake; the reed islands only grew fewer, and the lagoons on which they drifted wider and deeper blue, until there were no more islands.

Under a storm sky this landscape, too, could seem bleak and terrible, but now it seemed a wonderland, and the colours had the brilliance and clarity of fine enamel. Here in the shelter of the lagoons the reeds, golden as farmyard straw in the sunshine, towered out of water that was beetle-wing blue in the lee of the islands or ruffled where the wind found passage between them to the dull deep green of an uncut emerald. It was a landscape as weird as a Lost World, and through it flew birds as strange and unfamiliar in flight as pterodactyls; snake-necked African darters, pygmy cormorants, pelicans and halcyon kingfishers.

These last held for me the splendour of something once seen with the clear eye of childhood and long remembered, for the contrasts of the glorious electric-blue back and wings, the rich chestnut breast and crimson bill, had held me enthralled when I was at a preparatory school. The drawing master had one day placed upon my desk the stuffed skin of a halcyon kingfisher, and said, "If you think you can paint, try and paint those colours, boy, and be humble." Long and often I tried, and long and often he comforted me for my failure, and when the term was over and the holidays were to begin I found it on my pillow on the last night with a note that read, "I think you like it as much as I do, and you can see it more plainly. By which I don't mean I'm going blind."

There were familiar birds, too, a profusion of coots and diving duck dotted everywhere over the open water, and presently Thesiger said, "It's pretty uncertain where we shall have to spend tonight; we'd better shoot something if we don't want to go hungry. Shooting here is not a bit like any ideas you may have. It's a strictly unsporting business, and we expect—and get—at least two hundred per cent." (This was quite untrue, though I did not yet know it; it was a laudable effort to instil principle rather than fact.) "You get as many coots in a row as you can; you can only take single flying shots at duck and so on, and then God help you if you miss. It's food we're after; we can't carry enough cartridges for sport. Your reputation among these people will stand or fall absolutely by what you kill or don't kill, and they're all watching you."

As an encouraging introduction to shooting while sitting cross-legged in the bottom of a perilously wobbling canoe I felt that this could hardly have been improved upon, but when he solemnly handed me two cartridges with the words, "These are all you'll get", I realised that I had been wrong.

The crew steered for the nearest coots. It seemed to me that they displayed a really remarkable lack of intelligence; to begin with they approached the coots upwind, which in the shelter of the floating islands was not strong enough to blow the birds back over us when they became airborne; and they seemed to forget, too, that if they headed the *tarada* straight for their quarry I should have three men and the high curving prow of the boat between me and my target. For these reasons their first efforts were unqualified failure, and my two cartridges remained comfortingly intact and non-committal in the chambers. I was conscious, however, that with every passing minute their potential for disgrace was growing steadily.

At last the *tarada* made an oblique downwind approach to a restless bunch of coots in the lee of an island. At eighty yards they began to scutter off the water, but they had to turn into the wind to do so, and by the time they were fully airborne they were within range. They were sadly strung out, however, and I was surprised to see two fall to my first barrel. The rest were snatched by the wind and swirling away from me now, and the canoe caught a gust and began to turn away too; I realised that to turn one's body as one sits cross-legged one would require a torso that revolves from the hips like a tank turret. Suddenly I saw a little group of three coots that had not taken alarm until after my first shot, and were only now leaving the water. They made a solid little black patch in the air, and they fell as one bird.

Any possible pretence that two hundred per cent was customary or expected among Thesiger's crew was at an end; they were beside themselves with excitement and congratulation. Thesiger looked like a scoutmaster whose oldest and most oafish pupil has tied an accomplished and esoteric knot by accident. "Pity you aren't leaving us now; trouble about reputations won on flukes is that they're so shortlived."

To gather the most distant of the coots we had to leave the shelter of the floating islands and enter the troubled water of the open lagoon. Laden as the *tarada* was she had about four inches freeboard amidships. The coots were drifting before they were gathered; and one was wounded and led us a long chase on the open water. The *tarada* was drifting still farther while the boys decided the direction of Mecca before slitting the birds' throats, and by the time we were at last ready to go on we were farther from the shelter we had left than from the nearest island ahead of us. It was not much more than four hundred yards away, but the wind was tearing through in great gusts between the dotted islands away on our right that partially screened the open lake itself. Every yard of the distance was touch and go. Hassan had taken over the little hunting canoe from our pilot and was struggling along a gunshot away on our right; from where I sat the little craft was hidden completely, hull down between the sparkling blue and green waves, and only his torso showed paddling like a maniac. But his canoe was light and unladen, and he was in better case than we were, for we had seven men and heavy baggage aboard. We were shipping water over our side from every wave, not much each time, but already the aggregate was enough to determine the issue if the waves should get just that much bigger.

"Do these things float bottom up when they capsize?" I called to Thesiger.

"No. They sink like stones. I hope you've enjoyed your sight of the marshes."

It looked as if my reputation for shooting coots was secure after all; we would all be "leaving today". I am unable to swim a stroke, despite the fact that a large part of my life seems to have been spent on water, and none of our party could in any case have made that distance. Somewhere I had a kapok coat, but it was deeply buried in the baggage and this was no time to look for it. It seemed as good a place to drown as any other. Amara looked back from the bows once, and his face was very frightened.

The *tarada* wouldn't have floated for another fifty yards. We drove at the island like a drunkenly tilting lancer, and the great curved prow thrust far into the reeds and undergrowth of its face; one second there had been the cold bright water at our sides and the next we were sitting in a boat on dry land in a green bramble thicket with the tall golden reeds meeting overhead; the uncompromising anticlimax that is at the heart of all salvation.

Hassan in the hunting canoe had been unable to reach our island. To do so he would have had to turn his already waterlogged canoe quarter on to the waves. He had to keep the bows of the canoe turned into them and he made another island by the skin of his teeth, an island some hundred yards away and no bigger than a haystack.

We offloaded the *tarada* as fully and carefully as though this had been our destination, for, as Thesiger pointed out, we might well be there for days; moreover the *tarada* could not rescue Hassan from his ivory tower until it was emptied both of baggage and water. Our island was perhaps fifteen paces across, a jungle of giant reeds and bramble under-growth, and it drifted sluggishly across the blue lagoon, slowed to a snail's pace by its soggy sea-anchor of roots and turf. We made a clearing on the highest part of it, and the piled cases of ammunition and medicine gave us shelter from the wind. Amara and Sabeti set off to rescue Hassan in the now surprisingly seaworthy *tarada*, and Kathia and our late host began to cook.

Later during our long journey I used to look back with regret to that first somewhat perilous day in the marshes, for its freedom and spontaneity. Those may sound strange words to apply to some hours confined upon a drifting hulk of water-logged vegetation, but they were untrammelled by the rigid formulae of a guest-host relationship that was to become the rarely relieved pattern of all our wanderings—a double guest-host relationship for me, for I was the guest of a guest—and perhaps, too, since all decision had always to come from Thesiger, I was subconsciously pleased by something beyond his control. Freedom it seemed, and one could stretch one's body into attitudes too informal for the hearthside of an Arab home, and stand straight upon one's feet and feel the dignity of seeing the world from man's natural height.

The cooking was simple in the extreme. The skinned and split coots were impaled on cut reed stumps stuck into the ground at the edge of the fire. Our host who had come as pilot had brought with him some flour and a large fish; with the flour he made thick wads of stiff dough and jammed these on to more cut reeds about the flames; the fish he merely buried among the hot feathery ash of the reed fire. These proceedings did not, it must be admitted, produce the delicious meal that would make a suitable and traditional climax to their description; in fact the majority of civilised beings would, after the first mouthfuls, have preferred to go hungry. I, who habitually eat little and have few dislikes, found it mildly distasteful, but was hungry enough to swallow the great quantity of grey ash with which each item was coated as a rissole with breadcrumbs.

In the afternoon the wind moderated a little, not enough to give passage to the loaded *tarada*, but enough for the hunting canoe to struggle a little perilously about the lagoons. We were now without food and faced by the possible prospect of a night upon the island, so I went out with Hassan to look for more coots. No raft upon a great ocean can ever have seemed as insecure as did that hunting canoe to me; the bright blue waves broke right at the gunwhale, and the whole craft lurched wildly at every stroke of the paddle. Duck and coots were everywhere, but they were wild as the wind itself, rising far out and whirling down it like leaves in an autumn gale, over the gusty water and the high reeds that were blue and gold and glorious. At length a single tufted drake came scudding downwind high and wide and black-and-white in the cold sunshine. This seemed a target on which my reputation could not suffer irretrievably; furthermore he was crossing our bows and I did not have to attempt the impossible gymnastic of turning as I sat cross-legged. I did not expect to kill him, but I did; clearly Hassan had not expected it either, and his amazement was very gratifying.

There seemed nothing more in the lagoon, and we began to return. Then, in full sight of our island, we cornered a party of coots who could not make up their minds to rise into the wind towards us. We got within thirty or forty yards of them before they rose in a bunch. Exactly as I fired the first barrel the canoe tipped downward on that side and the shot passed a yard below them; then as it lurched upward the second barrel passed six feet over their backs. Hassan stared. Never, since as a boy at a covert shoot I missed fourteen pheasants in succession and in a remarkably conspicuous position, have I felt such agonising inadequacy; moreover no one had been depending on those pheasants for food.

Thesiger, waiting at the island, was not comforting. "Now I suppose we shall have to go on no matter what the weather's like; that little duck won't go far among seven people, will it? I told you about the dangers of a reputation built on flukes. Your name's mud among these boys now."

But the wind was dying when we left in the early evening. We skirted the fringe of Zikri, threading our way between the islands and through lagoons that gradually became smaller until we were once more among broad, ill-defined waterways with the reed-beds and bulrushes lower and less dense at our flanks.

As the sun began to set the wind dropped to a breath, and the confined water became glass calm, a mirror reflecting a sky from which all colour had ebbed, and even the sun sinking behind the sharply etched *cheval de frise* of reed tops was a blanched glare of light without hue. The great wilderness of water and reeds became pressing and mysterious as does a forest when the darkness comes, and with the hush of evening came the voices of the frogs.

Of all the strange sounds and sights of the marshes I think that I shall remember longest the tumultuous voices of the frogs, those million million voices that could turn the great marsh desert into a cauldron of sound seeming more limitless even than the falling horizons themselves. Later during our journey, when we were crossing the open water of some great lake and the giant reed-beds were a low golden wall in the distance there would be a temporary silence, a silence that seemed somehow uneasy because of the absence of a thing familiar; then, when the *tarada* was still half a mile from the reed-beds, it would creep back into the air like the distant murmur of a great concourse of men. At a quarter of a mile the tone would change to the jabbering of tens of thousands of monkeys; then, as the reeds closed round the canoe, it became a jagged wall of sound that cut one off from the open world outside.

There are several individual types of voice that fuse to compose that mad babel; and on that first evening, as the white sun sank and silhouetted the reed tops, the voices began individually before they gathered sweep and volume to engulf the night, so that for a minute or two it was possible to isolate the notes and search for comparison. The first voice of which I was conscious was loud and staccato and near at hand, a quick chatter indistinguishable from that of a magpie, ragged teeth of sound cutting into the gleaming bubble of low sun and water and the small liquid noises of the paddles. A second voice answered, a rhythmic double note exactly like a man sawing wood, harsh and rasping; a third was boisterous and expansive and could be mistaken for the quacking of a farmyard drake; a fourth would have passed in any Kensington drawing-room for the yapping of a hoarse Pekinese dog. Inherent in each of these voices, despite their differences, is some quality suggestive of remarkable enthusiasm, as though their owners were engaged upon some pleasurable and essentially exhilarating task. These diverse sounds fuse into a continuous and confused uproar, until only the very nearest have any recognisable form.

One seldom sees the owners of these voices except as a quick retiring ripple in the water; and I think the majority, anyway, are of no great size. Once, walking over partially flooded land near the perimeter of the permanent marshes, I picked up one of the many empty terrapin shells that lay on the short green turf. I was turning it over in my hands, when, from the hole where the living tortoise's neck should be, a small grey-green face emerged sharply. It gave a gruff and startled exclamation, regarded me glassily with the far-seeing and imperious eyes of a senior naval officer, and withdrew. I was peering after it when a second head, greener and larger than the first, popped out from the other end, emitted a single outraged gasp, and remained staring for a moment or two with a pulse beating angrily in its cheek. Nothing that I could do could persuade either of the occupants to show themselves again; I dropped the shell in a puddle and turned away. I had not taken more than two or three paces when I heard a chatter of insane laughter behind me, and whirled round in time to see a frog shoot out from each end of the terrapin and land with a plop in the shallow water. That was as near as I ever got to examining any member of the fabulous orchestra.

The daylight faded altogether from the sky, and the stars came out and were reflected in the water as chips of silver that wriggled like tadpoles in the ripple of the paddles. Now the marshes looked to me uniform and without landmarks, the reed tops showing barely darker than the sky, and the route we pursued among the winding waterways seemed arbitrary, our destination a pretence.

For more than three hours we moved through the darkness and the clamour of the frogs; then the reed-beds, whose surrounding presence we had felt rather than seen, became thinner, and suddenly there were lights ahead. It was my first sight of a marsh village at night, and it was not at first easy to make out what these lights were, flame-coloured and each shaped like a diamond on a playing card.

Nearly all marsh villages are built in the open water, a little away from the reeds so as to avoid the worst of the mosquitoes in summer, and each house is a tiny island of its own, an island built by staking its perimeter with cut reed-bundles in the shallow water and filling up the enclosed space with soggy vegetation until eventually its level is above that of the water. So little above the water, however, that in the dark the high triangle of light formed by the slit door is reflected on the surface of the lagoon without noticeable interruption of terra firma.

As we drew near to these strange houses and began to pass among them they appeared as a fleet of lit boats at anchor in a calm sea, the reed-railed buffalo-platform projecting from the rear of each like the round after-decks of a medieval galleon. Against the night sky showed the dark silhouettes of buffalo heads and horns and the high curving prows of canoes, and as we paddled soundlessly over the still water with the houses all about us we could see through their slit doors to firelit interiors where other buffaloes and their calves shared the warmth with the human family. Not galleons, perhaps, but Noah's Arks.

In one of these houses of Gabur we spent the night; but, as we arrived late and left very early the next day, it was not until we reached, in the middle of the following morning, a small village with the curiously flatulent name of Bumugeraifat that I formed any real impressions of a marsh community.

Bumugeraifat was in some sense Thesiger's headquarters, for he was perhaps better known here than anywhere else in the marshes; two of his crew had their homes here, and the villagers regarded him as their own property. It is a tiny village, each house its own island, some built on packed-down reeds and some on clay earth which may be no more than what the reed layers have become where a dwelling site has been inhabited for hundreds of years. The slit door of the house gives straight on to the water, separated from it, at the house at which we stayed both then and later in our journey, by two almost vertical feet of clay as slippery as vaseline. Directly below the eighteen-inch wide doorway the clay is black with ash thrown out from the hearth, and appears treacherously solid, but it remains only vaseline covered with charcoal, and to step ashore from the canoe remained to me, then and always, impossible without the grip and pull of a host's hand from the doorway.

Inside, the house differed little from that at Ramla, or from any other undistinguished house in all the marsh area, for the variations are small and somewhat unusual. It was a little more cramped and a little more untidy with broken reed fragments; and at the back, beyond the far half of the house where the womenfolk were cooking, extended the

61

short rounded buffalo platform that is the stereotype of every house in the permanent marshes.

The water buffaloes are by far the most important unit in the marshman's economy, and much of the family's life revolves around them. From excavations outside the marshes it has been possible to date the approximate year of their original introduction into the country from farther east as 3500 B.C.; more than five thousand years of segregation have changed them somewhat from the form of their Indian ancestors, and they are more like ponderous black aquatic cows than buffalo.

Their movements are, I think, slower than those of any other animal that I have ever seen, except perhaps—but only perhaps—those of a leisurely elephant; even their cud is chewed at a rhythm no faster than one movement of the jaw in three seconds. In the water, where they spend all their time when they are able, showing only a weary head or a length of dripping back like the keel of a long-submerged wreck in shoal-water, the buffaloes seem primeval, pachyderm, patient and wearily enduring; a little tragic too, reminiscent, perhaps, of forgotten news-reels of swimming cattle left derelict by flood. Their eyes are suffering, reproachful. Their voice is the voice of despair, tinged faintly with resentment, expressing only the emergence of the first beasts from the primeval swamps to the bewildering new world of land; it is not a moo or a bellow, but a very deep and infinitely prolonged groan. A mother defending her calf blows a long protesting puff of sweet-smelling breath; her whiskers vibrate tremulously.

The buffaloes are never killed for food; never, indeed, unless they are dying anyway of some disease, when the owner may try to secure the price of the hide while there is yet time. So timeless, so patient, is the *adagio* rhythm of their existence that one feels that they should somehow cheat death by pure inertia, and when they do die of one of the various diseases to which they are susceptible their bloated half-submerged carcases in the water, white-splashed with the droppings of pelicans and pygmy cormorants, have a strange pathos.

In fact they have little cause to complain, for their lives are passed in a rich and placid leisure immune alike from fear and frustration. They are maintained in privileged luxury for the sake of their milk and their dung; and of the two, safeguarding the bull calf from slaughter, the second is by far the more important. The marshmen drink the milk sour or as curds, or make from it butter churned by swinging the milk rhythmically in the suspended and dried skin of a sheep or a still-born calf, but it is in their dung that the true value of the buffalo lies. It is the marshman's only fuel other than the dangerous and quick-burning reeds, and his only waterproofing, cement-like, substance.

The dung is gathered—by the women only, for this is an unclean task and relegated to the proper quarter; no man would dream of touching buffalo dung—and shaped, if it is to be used for fuel, into plate-shaped pats, each bearing the spread imprint of a woman's left hand. When the pats are dry they are stacked as are peats in Scotland and Ireland, and the formation of the beehive-shaped stack is often of an intricacy and beauty that seem worthy of less transient an object.

A fire of buffalo dung is always laid and lit in the same way. Pat is built upon pat until a little dome-shaped oven is formed, with a side entrance like a wren's nest or the entrance to an igloo. Into this aperture is thrust a bundle of burning reeds, which is held there for as long as it may take for the walls and roof of the structure to become aglow. Then the reeds are taken away, and the buffalo dung smoulders with a smoke dense, acrid and suffocating. The marshmen profess indifference to these hell-fumes, and found my own streaming-eyed agonies a perpetual source of entertainment; nevertheless I noticed a certain amount of selection about seating positions on the leeward side of the fire.

As cement, for it is of a fine consistency and dries quite hard, the dung has infinite uses. It may patch leaking reed-and-mat walls of houses and shelters; it seals and roofs the upright cylinders of reed matting which are used to store grain; it sometimes cements the reed horizontal of a house to the reed matting that covers the whole structure; it may occasionally roof a whole building with circular tiles fitted in mosaic one against another. Its uses are so diverse, and for them it is so completely without possible substitute, that one's first reaction on learning that the value of a buffalo is about £25 is to think "All that dung for so little!"

Thus the buffaloes are, as it were, the marshman's lifeline, and they are cherished accordingly. The settled families of the marshes—in contrast to the nomadic tribes at their fringes who own great herds and move according to their requirements as the Lapps move with their reindeer—rarely have more than half a dozen buffaloes and often only two or three. At each dawn the buffaloes, who have been sleeping on the buffalo platform, or quite frequently round the fire with their owners, leave, infinitely slowly and wearily, their wallowing progress continually punctuated with despairing groans, for the distant reed-beds beyond the open water. For a long time they stand on the edge of the buffalo platform, groaning to each other of the infinite fatigue of the coming day, until at last the leader takes a ponderous pace forward and subsides into the water. This first subsidence, dependent as it is almost entirely upon gravity, appears the most rapid movement that they ever make, unless it be for the swishing of their tails when on dry land among the flies; for even their frequent matings seem performed with no great relish, as a ponderous and wearisome necessity, a tired effort to rid themselves of a physical discomfort.

Once in the water a deep lassitude once more descends upon the party, as if they had by now forgotten their intention, and they may wallow there with low notes of complaint for many minutes. The movements that at length remove them from the immediate vicinity of the house are so gradual as to pass practically unnoticed, but finally they are swimming, so low in the water that their noses seem held above it by a last effort of ebbing strength, their rolling eyes and despairing groans proclaiming that this is the end at last and that they are drowning.

So, patient and protesting and more or less submerged, they spend the day among the reeds and the bulrushes, grazing leisurely upon such green shoots as their ante-diluvian heads may find at eye level. Often, as we travelled, our *tarada* would come on them unexpectedly, heads with no visible bodies, and seeming the vaster for being at much the same level as our own. Outside the permanent marsh, where the floods come and go and the succulent new growth is often a foot or two under water, the buffaloes stand grazing with their heads submerged, often up to the horns, but it appears that this is a trick that requires learning, for the buffaloes of the true and deep marshes cannot take food beneath the surface.

These long-suffering animals are, however, far from dependent for a livelihood upon what food they may find for themselves during a day's leisurely sloshing and grazing through the shoulder-deep water. At about the same time as they have launched themselves querulously from the buffalo platform, their owners have put forth in their canoes for what is often the better part of a day's foraging in the reed-beds on behalf of their small herd. Often the whole family sets out soon after dawn, leaving their house guarded only by the indispensable watch-dog, and spends the day in the reed-beds cutting and loading into their canoes the green shoots that the buffaloes will eat at night. This green fodder is called *hashish* (literally grass) and its collection is the daily routine. On a still day in the marshes one may hear the *hashish* gatherers afar off, singing and shouting to each other through the golden curtain of the high reed forest, splashing and crackling as they force their craft deeper into the dense and brittle tangle of the sedge. Often they are wading waist deep as they drag their canoes beside them, the men and boys naked, with the water bright on the warm colour of their skins.

Late in the afternoon, when the sun has begun to light the distant walls of reeds to a flaring orange, the laden canoes begin to labour homeward to their island houses. The green fodder is spread on the buffalo platform, the buffaloes return in an orgy of despair from their fruitless and weary day, and settle down with grudging satisfaction to a ruminative and sappy night with the *hashish*. In the end they are little other than patient machines for processing the reeds into a suitable fuel. Once on dry land these exigeant creatures are easily tormented by mosquitoes and flies; and, perhaps because they are in a bovine way basically neurotic, the buffaloes quickly go down in condition if this nuisance is not dealt with. Here again their owners attend assiduously to their wants, and light small fires of dung above whose wreathing pale blue smoke the horned and wrinkled heads float disembodied as gods above a cloud of incense.

Despite their inimitable air of sloth the buffaloes give a strange impression of sentience and enlightened self-interest, and it is small surprise to learn that each cow answers her name promptly when she is called to be milked. The milking is customarily done by men, never by women, and Thesiger notes that the same is true of camels among the Bedouin of Southern Arabia.

I was never able to make out precisely what determined whether the buffaloes slept on the buffalo platform or round the fireside with the family. The calves, especially when string-muzzled at the time of weaning, often sleep right inside the house and near enough to the fire for their hair to singe and for sparks on their hides to be extinguished by the horny soles of bare feet. Sometimes the cows would be driven back protesting when they tried to force an entrance, but at other times their lumbering forms seemed to be accepted as a sort of natural obstacle, like a dry watercourse, to be circumvented with acquiescence. Accidents do sometimes result from this mingling of the ponderous with the essentially fragile, and Thesiger treated more than one child whose face as it slept had been stepped on during the night by a restless buffalo.

Soon after we had eaten I was sent out to shoot duck for the pot, taking with me four cartridges, and returned after some two hours with a bag whose entry in a game book would suggest that I had passed a somewhat whimsical afternoon's sport in a provincial menagerie. I had shot a tufted duck—so far so good—a red-crested pochard, a pelican, and a large water snake.

We had set out through a country of broad still lagoons on which rested wild and wary groups of duck and coot. I had learned my lesson about reckless expenditure of ammunition, and resisted firmly the urgent temptations of the boy who paddled my canoe to fire at the racing packs that whickered by two gunshots away. The red-crested pochard was alone and loath to leave the little lagoon he had made his own; he circled it and fell with a splash, lying with pathetic splendour of plumage on the smooth blue water. The tufted duck came next, and I felt that I had in some way atoned for my outrage by killing something so essentially dowdy and insignificant. The canoe rasped through a reed-bed and came out on another jewelled lagoon, upon whose surface rested a small flock of pelicans, uncouth yet stately.

For some reason the pelicans have not yet learned to fear man sufficiently, though small numbers of them are regularly killed by the Arabs, not for their flesh, which is left to waste, nor for any part of their plumage, but for the pendulous pouch of skin below the bill. It is this thin membrane, stretched and dried to a smooth parchment-like surface, that gives to the Marsh Arabs' drums and tambourines their peculiarly resonant note of urgency and hysteria. Often as the pitch of the drumming becomes faster and more fevered the membrane splits, and it is no unusual thing for a drummer to burst several drums in the course of an evening's entertainment. But the great white pelicans, so oafish and ungraceful on land or water but so irresistibly glorious in their flight, have either not yet learned to treat man as a serious enemy or they underestimate the length of his reach. They display nervousness, it is true, but often when well within gunshot. They turn curiously truncated rumps to their pursuers, paddling away with short nervous strokes and backward glances that have an air of chagrin and reproach.

I was anxious for purely subjective reasons that the pelican I was required to kill should be killed cleanly and instantaneously, but the danger of shot puncturing the pouch precluded aiming at the head. I compromised with the base of the neck, and was relieved when my vast victim collapsed without so much as a wing-flap. At the shot his companions rose with slow orderly strokes of their mighty wings, and while the boy was stripping the pouch from the dead bird the poor boobies came back to wheel round and round on motionless sails low over our heads, looking down wonderingly at the white inert carcase.

We were on our way home, paddling over still open water with a high reed-bed some thirty yards away on our right when I saw the snake, bright and coppery against the yellow reeds, coiled spirally round a bunch of their stems a foot or two above the water. Both the colour and the pose were quintessentially evil, and it did not need the feverish chittering of the Arab boy to tell me that we were in the presence of a known enemy. In moments of extreme tension the marsh people find it difficult, probably impossible, to whisper; their voices emerge as a rapid and febrile squeak, small, but with an impression of great force canalised through an infinitely narrow channel. The frustration inherent in the reduced volume finds simultaneous expression in magnified gesticulation, so that even the simple act of pointing becomes a series of rapier thrusts of the forefinger.

Just so the boy pointed out the snake to me after I had pointed it out to him, and as I brought the gun up to my shoulder the urgency of his injunctions to shoot was shrill as a flock of bats about my ears. It was not a very big snake, perhaps four or five feet long, and was unspectacular by comparison with the positive sea serpent of which I caught an uncomfortable glimpse a few weeks later.

I do not know whether these water snakes are all of one species, or even, with any certainty, their scientific name, for the Arabs hold them in such horror that to touch even a patently dead one creates a true panic. *Arbid* they are called by the marshmen, and they are said to be almost invariably deadly, killing in about twenty minutes after the bite. Thesiger had the previous year met a party returning from the funeral of a girl who had been killed by an *arbid*; they had carried the girl's body in their canoe to the place of burial, and when they had lifted it ashore a great gush of black blood had come from her mouth. This tale suggests that the *arbid* is of the viper tribe, whose venom kills by producing violent haemorrhage, rather than one of the colubrines, which act chiefly upon the nervous system and bring about death by respiratory paralysis.

Arbid undoubtedly grow to a very great size. Some weeks after I had shot this first snake as the conclusion to a curiously mixed bag, I had a fleeting and extremely close-up view of a snake whose size I should not, for fear of ridicule, care to estimate. We were travelling between villages in the fully laden *tarada*, with the crew of four canoe boys. Thesiger habitually accorded me the place of honour in the *tarada*, near to the stern of the canoe and facing forwards, while he himself sat opposite to me facing astern. There were two paddlers behind me, and two in the bows beyond him, but he was the only man who faced backward over the ground we had covered. We were passing through a narrow waterway with tall reeds pressing close at each side when my glance came quite by chance to rest on Thesiger's face. Just as it did so I saw his own gaze freeze with an expression of unbelieving horror on a point that seemed to me to be my own right elbow. His expression was so totally unfamiliar, so shockingly unlike his normal impassivity, that my head flicked round without a thought of asking him what he saw. About two feet from the side of the canoe, and a very little behind me, the last few feet of a great snake were slithering from the reeds into the water. From the character of the movements alone it was clearly the very end of the snake's body, yet the part that I was looking at was as thick as my forearm—which must, incidentally, have passed within touching distance of the head a second or two earlier. Thesiger had seen little more of the snake than I had, for it had not caught his eye until a fraction of a second before I had turned my head to see those last disappearing coils.

We were entertained that night by a dancer whose name I can no longer remember; it must, I think, have been a difficult name, for I referred to him then, and think of him now, as the Performing Flea. He must have been about eight years old. When at rest he looked a very small dreamy child with preternaturally large and luminous eyes like a lemur, and a face of gentle sadness. His appearance gave no more suggestion of his weird potentialities than does a stick of high explosive, yet when I think now of dancing in the marshlands it is that tiny whirlwind scrap of humanity that comes to my mind first.

Starlight and star-reflecting water through the slit doorway; inside, the focus of firelight, pale high-thrusting flames from a long column of reeds, and fifty-four people huddled round it in a space of four yards by four. The heads of those farthest from the fire were dim in the shadows. "Dance," said someone to the boy, and he made no half-hearted excuses. The centre of the circle shuffled back a little from the fire, leaving him a space which I judged to be no more than three feet by four.

The drums started, in slow rhythm at first, as the child began, two paces forward, two paces backward, without turning. *Ti-tumti-túm, ti-tumti-túm.* The child looked solemn, graceful, and controlled; his limbs moved with the sure precision of an adult, but there was as yet no hint of violence in the dance. Slowly the drums gathered speed and urgency and his feet kept pace with them quicker and quicker, *ti-tumti-túm, ti-tumti-túm, ti-tumti-túm.* His body lunged forward as though he would invade the crowd, and shot back from them again as though catapulted from their faces. The tempo grew faster and faster, and suddenly his shoulders began to keep time with his feet, each moving independently as though they were part of a machine driven by the same pounding crankshaft. Back and forth flew the feet, up and down shot the shoulders, and the huddled figures beyond the firelight roared out a chant in time with the drums while their clicking fingers smashed out the quickening rhythm. As the flames flickered down, the squatting holder of the reed bundle too absorbed to remember his task, the silhouette of the dancer was lost in his whirling *dish-dasha*; then, abruptly, as the reeds were thrust up again into the smouldering ash and the flame shot up, the outline of the dancer's body was thrown into sharp relief behind its thin covering, childish and slight as a tadpole. The boy brought another group of muscles into play, and his hips leapt and thrust in time with the flying feet and jerking shoulders, so that every part of the wildly capering figure was in separate and intricate movement. The dance was now frankly erotic. As the rhythm became faster still the boy would halt suddenly while first one and then the other shoulder shivered

71

and vibrated in convulsive spasms, or his hips writhed and shimmied in a paradox of controlled abandon. His eyes rolled and his tongue protruded; only the exquisite timing of his movements to the drums betrayed that he was not in epileptic seizure.

So caught did he seem in the demoniac rhythm of his own weaving that there seemed no possible end to the dance; here, it seemed, was the magic by which *le moment critique* became *l'heure critique*. For more than twenty minutes he maintained the pace without a falter, then suddenly he flung himself to the ground and lay jerking and twitching to the beat of the drums in a frenzied yet stylised pantomime of orgasm.

The drums stopped, and he rose in a storm of laughter and applause. Seated cross-legged again at the side of the reed hearth he was once more a staid and demure child, big-eyed, shy and wondering. His breathing was not perceptibly quickened, nor at the end of a twenty-minute encore was he more ruffled than if he had awoken from a light refreshing sleep.

In the morning we went out to shoot pig. Much as the water buffaloes are the mainstay of the marshmen's life, so the wild pig of the marshes are the greatest and most universal enemy. They are one of the commonest animals of the marshes, and they compare to the wild pig of Europe, or, I think, of India, as a Great Dane would compare to a terrier. They are probably the largest pig in the world. They are huge, evil tempered, and useless; for their flesh is unclean food to any Muslim, and their drab, well-camouflaged hulks lurk in every reed-bed. Here they build for themselves little soggy islands of broken reed on which to sleep, and often a party of *hashish*-gatherers, forcing its way through the reeds, stumbles unaware on a still form that becomes in a moment a raging tornado of slashing tusks that rip the flesh like knives and leave white bone open to the sky. Whether the pig actually kills or not is largely a matter of chance and whether the victim has fallen on his back or face, for after a sort of routine savaging of a few seconds the pig usually makes off.

The most serious injuries result when the victim has fallen on his back, exposing his face, throat, and stomach to the onslaught of the tusks, and these wounds are often fatal. But because the pig never stays to make sure that his enemy is dead there is always a good chance of escape, and a great many of the Ma'dan carry scars of past gorings that they have survived. Pig will even attack a large canoe if it surprises them while sleeping, and Thesiger told me that he had seen the bows of a thirty-six foot *tarada* completely stove in in this way.

It is small wonder that the marshmen hate the wild pig, and kill them by any possible means. Thesiger, who is a very good shot with a rifle, had earned the gratitude of many villages many times over, for he had killed literally hundreds of pig during his years among the Ma'dan, and they now felt it to be part of his natural function, like the doctoring of their diseases. But firearms are not universal, and ammunition rare by comparison to the great number of pig, so that the marshmen's means of attack are strictly limited. They say— though I never saw it done myself, and it contrasts strangely with the terror I have seen them display toward a moribund boar struggling in deep water—that when a pig is swimming a man will dive into the water and drown it by imprisoning the hind feet. Many pigs, too, are killed by spears and clubs as they swim; one village we passed through claimed to have killed as many as a hundred and forty pigs in a year. The young fallow-spotted piglets they slaughter unmercifully and unpleasantly, for they are the enemy shorn of his weapons, and can show no fight. In these circumstances the marshmen show an active cruelty no different from the treatment of any other scapegoat elsewhere, but difficult superficially to distinguish from their normal total indifference to animal suffering. They do not at any time or in any way identify themselves with animals, and this utter callousness can give a misleading impression of active sadism. Every animal that a Muslim ever kills must, if it is to be eaten, be bled to death with a slit throat and its head pointing towards Mecca, and this, if it is a large animal, can be a peculiarly revolting procedure. Since all reaction to animal situations can only be a result of identification with the animal, and since the identification is entirely absent, there is no inhibition about display of other emotions that may be aroused; amusement, for instance, at the grotesque movements of a wounded animal. They can detect no element of pathos. I have seen several Arabs roaring with genuine laughter at the weird gyrations of a wild duck with a partially slit throat. Quite a different element creeps in when the wounded animal is a pig, but the nuance is difficult to detect.

In the same way, a pig hunt is imbued with a subtle intensity that is foreign to the pursuit of any other quarry. The feelings and the recollections of those pig hunts are with me now as I write, the remembrance of something stealthy and atavistic, something intent and destructive.

Paddling silently along the edge of the reed-beds and listening. Heads cocked on one side, strained, alert. The minute liquid tinkle of the water-drops that fall from the dipped paddle as the canoe slides forward soundlessly. The unfamiliar croak of a purple gallinule and a faint crackling of dry sedge deep in the undergrowth. The sudden sound of an eagle stooping, the air vibrating in the stiff pinions like a rush of winds in the reeds. The paddles thrust noiselessly, and the bright drops trill back from them on to the blue lagoon water. The canoe rasps and grates through a belt of reeds, forcing its way through to a new lagoon; the noise seems outrageous, deafening. At eye level is stretched the untenanted web of a spider, filled with a hundred flies; the sun glints on their green metallic bodies splayed on the deserted net. The canoe leaves the reeds, the din stops very suddenly, and one is again in a world of silence. Overhead the sea eagles wheel on the blue sky and a kingfisher scintillates dazzlingly across the bows. Everyone is listening, listening for some small sound which will be unrecognisable to me when it comes.

For this, the sound of the enemy, the marshmen's ears have an almost incredible sensitivity and selectivity. During the short time that I was among them, one rustle in the reeds remained to me much like another; the small sounds that came from the unseen inhabitants of the reeds seemed undifferentiated. But to the Ma'dan each, however small, produces a clear picture of what is taking place out of sight.

They ignored a heavy splashing and crackling that I thought could only be a startled pig; then, seconds later, they stiffened at some sound inaudible to me. Fingers pointed feverishly, Thesiger stood up amidships in the canoe and unloosed the safety catch from his rifle. Even the tinkle of water dripping from the paddles seemed to be stilled, and we moved over the mirror-smooth surface in utter silence. Thesiger took aim at something I could not see, in a low reed-bed some fifty yards away to our left.

The slam of the rifle was followed instantly by squealing and crashing in the sedge, and a hairy brown shape somersaulted backward into the water. The pig floundered and plunged, swimming in a tight circle like a cat chasing its tail. Its shattered lower jaw dangled from the head, gushing blood into the blue water until the surface closed over it and only a patch of scarlet was left. A terrible and revolting animal, dying a terrible and revolting death.

> If every violent death is tragedy
> And the wild animal is tragic most
> When man adopts death's ingenuity,
> Then this was tragic. But what each had lost
> Was less and more than this, which was the ghost
> Of some primeval joke, now in bad taste,
> Which saw no less than war, no more than waste.

We emerged soon after this on to the great lake of Daima, a vast expanse of pale satin blue with its confining wall of reeds far off and small. As we came out through the widening channel into the open water I saw a fishing spear thrown for the first time.

The five-pointed fishing spear is, together with a short metal-headed club and a curved knife whose sheath is a buffalo horn, part of every marshman's equipment. Shaped like a trident, but with five prongs, the iron head is mounted on a pole some ten feet long, and it is with this alarming—but, in its proper context, inefficient—weapon that the greater number of fish in the marshes are killed. It is used against pig, too, and occasionally against human beings, and against these solid and visible targets it is deadly, though it is most commonly thrust at random into the water at the foot of the reed stems where fish may be lurking.

More occasionally it is flung, as it was now. Amara threw down his paddle, seized the spear that lay beside him, and stood up in the bows. Some ten or fifteen yards ahead there was a very faint ripple on the smooth surface. Amara hurled the spear with all his strength; it struck the centre of the ripple and stuck quivering with two feet of its length hidden in the shallow water. No one, I think, except possibly myself, expected there to be anything on the end of the spear when we reached it, but there was; a fish little more than nine inches long and firmly impaled by three prongs of the spear. If I had left the marshes then I should have returned with tales of the marshmen's fabulous skill with the spear, of a target nine inches by three hit squarely at forty-five feet from a moving canoe. Alas, it was like my own reputation, so soon to be temporarily redeemed, for the mass killing of coots; it could not last.

Far out in the middle of the lake lay a long solid line like land, perhaps a mile of it, and dark as charcoal. As I looked at this my eye was caught by something above it, something hurtling downward like a diving aircraft, and then another and another. A line of white foam suddenly edged the dark strip that looked like land, and a muttering roar like the undertow of a wave came to us across the mile of still water. The dark line was formed of coots, many, many thousands of them, bunched together under the repeated attacks of five eagles. The eagles could not strike while the coots remained on the water, and again and again they hurtled downward, trying to panic the great throng into taking wing. Under each attack the whole mass spread their wings and scuttered forward for a few yards, driving a frothing wave before them, and as the eagle pulled out of his dive and began to climb again the coots bunched tightly together so that one could not have dropped a pin between them. Here was an occasion on which the meanest shot might indeed have fulfilled Thesiger's demand for two hundred per cent on cartridges fired.

We started off across the lake towards them, but before we had got halfway the eagles had grown bored and dispersed. Two of them came sailing by low over our heads; these were the white-tailed sea eagles that breed in the reed-beds, and, when their young are in the nest, often terrorise the *hashish*-gatherers who trespass on their territory. The others were smaller and very dark; I hesitate to try to pin the correct label on any animal or bird from the marshlands, since the only living creature I brought home proved to be totally new to science. During the winter and early spring eagles are one of the commonest of all birds in the marshes, and there is rarely any moment when, if the sky is not a mere strip between the towering reed tops, there are not half a dozen or more in view. They seemed to me to be of a bewildering number of species. They are not killed by the Arabs, and so have little fear of man; like the cynical-looking black-and-white crows, they perch as do reed warblers on the bending stems of the giant reeds, and often allow a canoe to pass close beneath them.

Now that the eagles were far off the coots had become less densely packed, though they still appeared as a mass solid enough to walk upon for perhaps half a mile, and they had less fear of rising. They began to scutter off the water when we were some eighty yards away, and a gigantic smother of fine spray filled the air, multihued like a rainbow. Had they been overhead they would literally have cut off the light like a canopy, but they were well out to our right. There were so many of them, and their places in the air were so instantly filled by those behind them, that it was difficult to see whether anything at all fell to my shots, but when the whole great concourse had gone and the rainbow mist of their going still hung on the air there were no less than nineteen left on the water.

I lost all illusions I had held as to the marshmen's accuracy with a fishing spear. Some of these coots were wounded and diving, and these we had to chase with the canoe. Again and again Amara or Hassan flung the spear at a coot no more than three paces from the boat, and again and again they missed by feet. A more inept performance could hardly have been contrived.

We ate as we had eaten on our first day in the marshes, on a drifting island with the high reeds leaving only a sky-patch above us, charred coots, dough bread, and Amara's memorable fish. To this was added some date treacle, of which we were the second or possibly third thieves. The keen eyes of the canoe boys had spotted it hidden in a thicket of reeds, several basket-work jars of a thick glutinous substance not unlike black treacle. It was pronounced to have been stolen and concealed, so now it was stolen again.

The wind sprang up again before we got home that night, and in the house at Bumugeraifat the lee-side of the fire was suffocating with the smoke of the buffalo dung, the windward side swept by an icy gale through the gaps in the reed wall.

Those were our first three days in the permanent marshes, and it was ten days before we came back to them, for the next morning we left for Rufaia, a village on the edge of the cultivating country, which was the home of Amara and Sabeti. We had in three days passed through the central marshes—those, that is, lying to the west of the Tigris—from south to north, and were now at their northern extremity, some twenty miles south of the town of Amara. The waterways, even outside the perimeter of the permanent marsh, remain the arteries of all transport, and the change is gradual. The reeds grow shorter and more scattered, then cease altogether; the waterways become clogged and red-brown with mud. When the wind blows, the water of these channels takes on a strangely individual colour, which is at first difficult to identify. The surface becomes ruffled into a formation like little conical sand dunes; one side of each dune is a warm buff, the colour of the cloudy water, and the other is turquoise-blue reflecting the sky. Thus the whole, which seems an indefinable and absolutely characteristic colour, is in fact a mosaic of two colours whose symmetry in movement gives the effect of being one.

We turned from these muddy waterways into narrower channels cut between rice fields, and there were earth banks at our sides where crabs' claws and carapaces and the shells of big mussels were crusted like decorated stucco.

The rice country is flat and featureless, and everything is of one colour. When the reed matting is first laid on the houses it is bright corn-gold, but it soon weathers to a dull mud-grey, and becomes part of a background where all is dun, the ground, the reed houses, even the cows and sheep; only the young thrusting shoots of the rice itself are a tender green. It is a land of monotony, a land, for me perhaps, of agoraphobia, for I never felt at ease in it, and when we were outside the marshes I longed always to return to them.

It was when we came to Rufaia that night that I realised how greatly my seldom-varying posture of the past three days had affected my muscles. When I climbed up the mud bank to the group who awaited us my legs felt unfamiliar; I

79

straddled and staggered like a new-born foal, and my head felt too high in the air. Every bone and muscle from the waist downward ached and creaked in unison. I wanted nothing but that the ten or twenty yards between us and the house should prolong itself into as many miles, but I was on my feet for less than a minute, a minute of dust storm and bare horizons, before I was again seated cross-legged on the floor of a reed house.

Here, in a village from which two of Thesiger's crew came, the house filled quickly, and the medicine chest was in immediate demand. As at Ramla there was too much dust and wind for the patients to congregate outside, and they were treated at one end of the little house. It seemed mystic, ritual; the orange spotlight of the dipping sun breaking through gaps in the reed wall to bring fine focus to an eye, the curve of a lip, a dapple over a moving hand. When the sun had gone and the throng was lit only by the flickering light of the buffalo-dung fire, Thesiger's form bending over a patient seemed huge and menacing as that of a witch-doctor, the shroud of the blanket that he wore as a shawl casting on the arching walls a great bird-like shadow with flapping wings.

At this time the physical ills of the people still made a vivid impression upon me, for, describing that hour, I find that I wrote in my notebook:

"The number of people with only one eye.
       "   "   dog bites.
       "   "   pig gores.
       "   "   miscellaneous but horrifying ills.
Four noseless faces tonight."

As time went on I came to accept these things as part of the milieu, so that at last to eat from the same rice bowl as a leper with only one finger left on his right hand seemed worthy only of a brief sentence, a jotting under a date.

I remember it as a restless night. Through the hours of darkness dogs barked and growled round the thin reed walls of the house, and about three in the morning began an interminable conversation between a few elders who squatted round the embers of the fire. It was the first of seemingly endless debates about Amara's marriage to Sabeti's sister, the arrangement of bride price and date, the anticipation and prevention of disputes that might arise. All through the night it dragged on while Amara, frankly indifferent, slept within touch of them, his handsome arrogant young face purged by sleep and the dim light of an habitual expression often near to cruelty.

Clay oven and vessel

Chapter Five

SHEIKHS are for the most part much what Europeans traditionally expect them to be. They tend to be stout men, they wear flowing robes—often elaborated with much gold braid—and flowing head-dresses. They squat cross-legged, so that their legs look exaggeratedly short and small in proportion to their bodies. They are accustomed to having their hands kissed often and obsequiously, and look used to getting their own way. Some of them appear despotic, some jolly and benign; a few seem vacuous and evil. Usually they are a little pop-eyed.

They rule over a greater or lesser area of land which may be rich cultivating ground with an intricate irrigation system, or some permanent marsh unimprovable except by the millions of dollars derived from oil fields. The word sheikh implies little more than "squire" or "laird"; a heritable title involving status and responsibility. All land in Iraq belongs ultimately to the State, but the sheikhs hold their traditional acres in a kind of feu from the government, and it is they who are responsible for the welfare, administration, and peace of their people.

When, before the First World War, this land was under the Ottoman Empire, tribal warfare was intense and constant, and was encouraged by the Turks in order to keep the tribes in too weak a state for united revolt. Serious fighting came to an end during the period of British rule, and the sheikhs' hereditary status as tribal leaders in warfare is at best anachronistic, their very existence but a transitional stage in the fulfilment of an idea that may never be completed. The basic problem of the country is water, and its fair control and distribution is the most convincing reason for maintenance of the sheikhs in *status quo*. When a sheikh is responsible for land it is in his interest to see that all his cultivators receive water for their crops at the right time; each sheikh or his *wazir* knows the local aspect of this problem, and how and when each parched rectangle of land may receive its vital supply. Ideally, some government official might effect the distribution with an equal impartiality, but they could learn only from the sheikhs' agent, and this apprenticeship would involve, to them, an impossible loss of caste.

The controller, too, has no incentive to see that each cultivator gets water when he requires it unless he himself benefits; it is too easy and tempting to accept a bribe by which he who pays most gets the water, necessity notwithstanding. Sometimes the maintenance of a local water supply involves the building of huge dams—an extremely difficult, complicated, and often dangerous process—which is made possible only by a feudal edict from the sheikh, uniting under plain compulsion a group of people who would never voluntarily co-operate with each other. By the present policy the government is taking half the land from the sheikhs and dividing it among the cultivators; who then will guarantee to each the water without which his land must become infertile and his family *déraciné*? The Biblical sin of Onan was the sin of a people who lived in a waterless land, the guilt of the diversion of all true fertility.

From the very earliest times the conquerors of the flat lands of the Tigris and Euphrates have recognised the flowing water as life-blood, without which all existence would cease. They did not strike at the great arteries and veins, allowing the liquid to seep away into futility; they struck at the heart itself by killing or deporting the *wazirs* who knew where the water must go for life to continue. There are great areas now that have remained desert since the times of the early conquerors, their peoples extinct or drifted without legend to tell of distant migrations from the terrors of drought in the flat lands.

Not all sheikhs, however—and more especially this is true of those who have had contact with the urgent western culture which is beginning, inevitably, to invade their perimeter—fulfil their hereditary responsibilities. A sheikh held land irrigated entirely by water pumps. Europeans taught him their customs; he became a gambler. He could not wager his land, which belonged ultimately to the State, but he gambled away the only movable assets upon it, his water pumps. The winner came and took them away, and the land became a desert, and the people left and there is no memory of where they went. An outraged government intervened to take the land from the sheikh, and gave it to a worthy and wealthy merchant who reinstalled the pumps and brought in fresh cultivators to work the ground. A feud then started between the merchant and the evicted sheikh, who claimed that his land had been appropriated. A skirmishing civil war began and the State had once more to intervene.

Few, if any, rich sheikhs actually live in the permanent marshes, though their jurisdiction encloses, piecemeal, every Ma'dan tribesman. They dwell on the dry banks of the great waterways at the marsh's edge, in embattled stone fortresses, waited on by a bevy of African slaves who have acquired in the course of generations both their religion and the benefits of a tolerance that amounts in effect to racial equality. The slaves' children grow up playing with the sheikh's children, and few if any of them would voluntarily leave the service of their masters. They are privileged and protected, and live in a security greater than that of the tribesmen themselves. Another type of sheikh lives within the perimeter of the true marshes, whose status is due rather to inherent quality than to inherited riches. These men often own no land; they or their fathers have been chosen by the community as suitable leaders in the settlement of disputes ranging from blood-feud to petty theft.

The fortresses of the feudal sheikhs are of a uniform type,

squat and expressionless; and, in all those that I saw, of a uniform interior decrepitude. Each contains a European type reception room, whose general introduction dates from the later part of the British occupation, and is now rarely used except for the entertaining of government officialdom. It is a long narrow room, round whose walls are ranged, shoulder to shoulder, heavy and identical arm-chairs and sofas, mass-produced in Basra and Baghdad. The room is usually deep in dust, the walls peeling and the paint cracking, and from the ceiling dangle weak and naked electric light bulbs as bleak as a whore's smile. It was in such a room that we were invariably received, and as I never penetrated to the residential portions of the forts I retained only impressions of decay, though essentially a hospitable decay; cool shade from the heat outside and the rare privilege of relaxing one's limbs into the postures to which they had been trained.

Near to his fort every sheikh, and many a man of lesser importance, maintains a *mudhif*, or guest-house, the vast nissen-shaped house of reeds, at which any passing stranger may partake of his hospitality. A halfway house, as it were, between *mudhif* and fort is the *sarifa*, a smaller rectangular reed building designed for the entertainment of a smaller number of more intimate friends, but these are by no means general.

Nearly every family of important sheikhs is related to every other by marriage, much as are many dukedoms in England, so that after we came that evening to the *mudhif* of Abd el Nebi bin Dakhil, a scion of one of the greatest families, I found that the *mudhifs* that we visited subsequently were often the property of his uncles, nephews, grandfathers or cousins, shoots of a genealogical tree so bewilderingly luxuriant that it would have required drastic pruning to become comprehensible.

We had left Rufaia through narrow hard-banked irrigation channels running between strips of date palm and rice fields over which flocks of rooks strutted and squawked beneath a clouded sky; by comparison with the brilliant colours and weird birds of the deep marshes the scene appeared common-place and insipid, almost European. We turned into broader channels some fifty yards wide, the water pale buff and opaque, fringed with willow and tamarisk and dotted irregularly with houses, whose baying, snarling watchdogs forced our crew on the towpath into a constant and capering rear-guard action.

The clouds had cleared as the sun began to go down, and we turned into the last wide stretch to see the *mudhif* as a dark dome against a yellow sky painted with stylised egret-plumes of black and crimson. The black feathers were spread and tufted as though applied with an almost dry brush; they were as dark as the *mudhif* itself, as the featureless land, as the single palm tree that jabbed the horizon far off; almost as dark as the high claw of the *tarada*'s prow, cutting the clear yellow distances on which they drifted. Nowhere have I seen sunsets at once as strange and as beautiful as those that flared nightly over the plains of the Tigris and the Euphrates; in the cultivating lands their colours, I think, appeared more intense by contrast with the daytime monotony of the drab earth and the dead reeds of the houses, but these sunsets avoided, somehow, the extravagant and ominous vul-garities of the north, where every colour on the palette is slashed together in Wagnerian tumult.

Though every day's end over the flat lands seems sharply individual, and the same hues and combinations are rarely repeated, there is a sequence of light changes that remains constant. At first the sun is low and blinding. Figures and reed houses on the river banks are focused as with an orange spotlight against an eastern horizon of smoky violet; a homing flight of pelicans is lit from below as though their breasts wore shields of brass. Above them the night is already dull blue and immense, stippled with stars. The sun sinks abruptly below the horizon, and the sky it has left is a band of harsh orange-yellow, merging above first into green and then into dull blue; it is separated only by a finger's width of dark land from the reflecting water. Slowly the yellow smoulders out into a carmine stripe, the distance becomes dim, and the stars become brilliant overhead. Against the still pallid water move the high prows of the canoes, their thin scimitar curves cutting into the embers of the horizon sky.

It was in this melodramatic light of the last moments before the sun was obscured by the thin horizon-stripe of land that we came to Abd el Nebi's *mudhif*. All the light had gone from the land, but the great arched building of drab and faded reeds blocked the horizontal rays until it glowed as yellow as gold.

Abd el Nebi had succeeded his father Dakhil as a result of an accident whose tragedy and confusion extended, as does all violent death in the marshes, far beyond its moment. Dakhil had been a close friend of Thesiger's, who had stayed regularly and often at this *mudhif*; and at length Dakhil asked him to come instead to the stone fort, saying that he should by now consider himself to be one of the family. The morning after Thesiger had stayed for the first time in the fort, Dakhil proposed a day's duck-shooting in the marshes with a number of other guests, including a certain Aboud, his nephew and son-in-law.

On their way out to the shoot Thesiger noticed a number of twelve-bore cartridges marked "LG"; and, not having seen them before, asked Dakhil what they were. He replied that they were duck-shot, and in curiosity Thesiger opened one. Six vast lead pellets trickled out into his hand.

"Someone will get killed by these," he said, "they are for shooting large animals such as pig. They would be terribly dangerous to use at a shoot like this." But Dakhil's attention was distracted, and he paid no heed.

The party separated among the reeds, each gun in a small

canoe with one paddler, and out of sight of each other. A few duck were soon on the move and there was some desultory shooting. Once Thesiger heard the peculiar hollow echo that comes from a shotgun fired straight in the direction of the hearer, and remarked that someone was shooting dangerously.

At about noon a shot was fired not far from Thesiger, and suddenly the voice of Dakhil was crying: "You have killed me, you have killed me!" His nephew Aboud appeared in terror from behind a reed-bed some seventy yards away, protesting incoherently that he had not known his uncle to be there. He did not wait to see whether or not he had killed; fear overrode all other considerations, and he fled wildly through the sheltering reeds, urging on his terrified paddler.

It is thus among the tribesmen that a blood feud begins. A life, even if taken accidentally, must be paid for by a life, if not by that of the killer himself then by that of a male blood relation, and that in turn by a man of the blood of that killer, and so the whole pathetic rigmarole goes on until at length it is settled by a payment of women. Tribal murder does not receive the normal sentence from the State, and its penalties are reduced still further if the act has been committed in hot blood, that is to say within a certain number of hours of the killing which it avenges.

In the eyes of this community there was only one possible course of action for Aboud to have pursued. His father should have taken him to Dakhil's father Mehsin—a powerful sheikh and one of the great figures of Southern Iraq—and said to him: "Here is my son on your mercy—he has killed your son in an accident; take his life in return if you wish." Then, they say, he would have been shown mercy.

Thesiger approached Dakhil's canoe within moments of his being hit; he saw Dakhil collapse and the paddler contrive miraculously to keep the canoe afloat. Dakhil was unconscious now, and over his left breast there was blood on his shirt; opening it, Thesiger found a puncture mark on the nipple.

He recovered consciousness while they were carrying him home, and sent urgently for his son Abd el Nebi, who, barefooted on the thorny ground at the edge of the waterways, could not keep up with the party. Those who carried Dakhil would not risk waiting, so the dying man sent word back to his son that whoever fired the shot must be returned unharmed to his father.

Once back at the fort, there was much argument as to where Dakhil should be sent, but by now there was in any case little hope. Finally a special plane was sent to fly him from Amara to Baghdad, but it did not arrive until some thirteen hours later. Dakhil died in Baghdad twenty-six hours after the shot had been fired.

Meanwhile the terrified Aboud had fled to his father, who, instead of taking him to the father of the dead man and throwing themselves on his mercy, surrendered his son to the government authorities, a treacherous defiance of tradition that could only expect hatred in return. He employed official channels and lawyers, and Aboud was finally sentenced to three years' imprisonment, which is the customary penalty for tribal murder.

Mehsin wanted vengeance. Another of his sons had been killed in mysterious circumstances, and his only surviving heir was not the apple of his eye. He mourned for Dakhil, saying, "Now I have no son left worthy of the name," and he awaited Aboud's release from prison.

At last Aboud's sentence was ended, and he at once received word from Mehsin saying that he would be killed if he came back to the area. Terrified, he appealed to the government, who sent him back saying that the State would be responsible for his life. Mehsin raised the tribesmen, and Aboud's canoe was ambushed and sunk before ever he reached home. Aboud escaped, and bolted back once more to the government authorities.

Mehsin disclaimed responsibility for the outrage, saying that he had never given the order, but his son was imprisoned for a while and the incident caused some loss of face. This time Aboud was sent back to live beside a police post, without cultivators or an appreciable amount of cultivable land. Threats reached the pedlars and travelling merchants, and none dared sell their goods to him. I do not imagine that an insurance company would give much for his life.

The atmosphere beneath the dim and stately arches of a sheikh's *mudhif* is, for a guest, very different from that of a village house. As time wears on the *mudhif* fills, it is true, but for the most part with elderly and dignified Arabs who squat cross-legged in silence. Speech when it comes is gentle and desultory; the beads click slowly and aimlessly between their fingers like the clucking of hens in a summer farmyard. The blue smoke curls up like incense from the burning dung at the coffee hearth; overhead it has given to the reed arches of the *mudhif* a patina as rich and glossy as old mahogany.

The people drifted away early, since there is rarely singing or dancing in so august an establishment, and as we lay down to sleep swarms of bats flitted among the dim columns above us, casting huge upward shadows on the arch-tops. Near to the door the faces of four black slaves were lit alone in the darkness by the flame of a Lux lantern; they squatted by the hot embers with their rifles across their knees, and the grotesque whirling shadows swooped over them like vampires.

We lunched the next day at the fort of Mehsin's brother, Jabir; in this atmosphere of internecine strife it was not surprising to learn that the two were not on speaking terms with one another—or rather were said to be "shouting insults at each other across the river".

The day was marked for me by an incident of painful comedy. I had brought with me from England a fishing spear gun of the type commonly used in conjunction with a Schnorkel mask by holidaymakers on Mediterranean shores. The gun was not mine, and I had never used it; nor, indeed had its owner, who had confided to me that in circumstances of peculiar chagrin he had discovered his utter inability to load it. It was before these toys had become popular, and they were still a novelty on most *plages*. He had been reclining on the sand of an Italian beach with the shiny and as yet untried object beside him when a group of Italians approached and asked if they might look at it. They examined it with animation and interest, and inquired if it were really possible to spear fish under water with this weapon. Its owner assured them that this was the case. They remarked that it must require much skill, and my friend replied that this, too, was so. They tempted him with admiration and flattery; in a few minutes he had sketched in a light picture of gaudy gurnards and ink-squirting octopuses impaled by his deadly aim deep down in the jewelled garden. Almost diffidently they inquired how to load this beautiful toy.

He knew the principle but had never tried the practice. At the muzzle end of the gun were two big loops of finger-thick rubber, and these had to be stretched back by brute force until they engaged in two corresponding notches at the butt-end of the barrel. He did not anticipate any particular difficulty, and with an easy condescension he reached for the weapon to demonstrate the procedure.

Under the amazed and then frankly amused eyes of the Italians he strained and tugged at one of the rubber loops without being able to stretch it halfway toward the notch for which it was destined. He was dripping with sweat and scarlet with effort and embarrassment when after many minutes he had to explain that it was not in fact with this gun but with another that he had decimated the shoals. The gun returned to England unfired, and was kept where it could arouse no moody memories of humiliation.

There was time to put away at Jabir's fort by the edge of the river, and I decided to see whether I would fare better than the gun's owner; making very clear to the onlookers, however, that I had neither loaded nor fired it before today. Owing to the sprouting curve of white rubber that grew from its muzzle the gun had early been christened by the canoe boys the Father of the Horns—(in the same way they refer to a particularly verminous house as the Father of Fleas, or to a hospitable sheikh who kept a lamp of invitation burning before his *mudhif* as the Father of the Light)—and they were no less curious than I to see just what the horns could do.

Whatever else they could do it did not seem at first as if they could be made to stretch a fraction of the required distance. I sat on the bank and jammed the pistol butt of the gun into my stomach and tugged until my muscles were aching and my stomach bruised, until at last, breathless, I slipped first one loop and then the other into their retaining notches. When I had done this I put on the safety catch and rested.

Hassan became impatient, and fetched some pats of buffalo dung to throw into the water as targets. At last I felt ready for a trial demonstration.

He tossed a pat on to the opaque yellow surface a little upstream of me so that it would be carried past me on the current some twenty feet away. I removed the safety catch, took careful aim along the barrel with the metal pistol grip a couple of inches in front of my nose, and pulled the trigger.

Something hit the bridge of my nose with shattering force, and I was knocked over flat on my back. I began automatically to get to my feet again, and saw as I did so that my shirt was covered with blood and that it was splashing heavily from my nose. I fumbled in my pocket for a handkerchief, and as I touched my nose I heard the bones inside clicking like a box of dice. Thesiger was hovering between concern and uncontrolled laughter; and the tears were streaming down my face as uncheckable as the blood.

At this point an agitated slave rushed up to us with cries of sympathy and dismay, and on hearing that my nose was broken exclaimed in great agitation that he would bring medicaments at once. Thesiger indicated his vast medicine chests that were stacked within a few feet of us, but the slave's goodwill would take no denial and he hurried off into the fort. A second or two later he came panting forth and with reassuring smiles pressed into my hand a small bottle labelled in English "Squibb's Mineral Oil". This struck both Thesiger and myself as excruciatingly funny, and I began to giggle so helplessly that the slave clearly thought my reason to have been affected by the blow.

When my nose had stopped bleeding and I had cleaned up my shirt as well as I could, I decided to try the gun again. This time I held it well away from my face with my arms braced. The shock against my tense muscles made it very easy to understand why my nose had broken. The spear shot merrily if inaccurately on its way, but as it did so I was conscious of a searing pain in my left thumb. This time the flying line connecting the spear to the gun had carried away with it an inch-long strip of skin. I returned the outrageous weapon to the *tarada*, uncomforted by a further offering of Squibb's Mineral Oil.

In the afternoon we left Jabir's *mudhif* downstream to visit his grandfather the great Mehsin, but when we arrived at his fort on the river bank he was in the act of stepping into a great high antediluvian-seeming motor launch to visit his son Ali. We abandoned the *tarada* to the canoe boys and travelled with him, our mountainous conveyance hammering and vibrating down-river between packed villages orange in the glare of light that comes before sunset.

It was in this same weird stage lighting that we came to Ali's *mudhif*. It leaned drunkenly at an angle of forty-five degrees, its foundations undermined by floods three years before, and had been long since due for repair. Ali had planned this the previous year, but had been thwarted by the total destruction of the reed crop which should have rebuilt it. There had been a cataclysm of nature, a hail storm of unprecedented violence, whose stones had been bigger than golf balls, killing many men, decimating the birds, and smashing down the giant reeds until they lay flat over the marshes like laid corn at the end of a wet and windy English summer.

Slaves carried into the *mudhif* several of the heavy arm-chairs from the reception room of the fort, and in one of these Mehsin sat near the entrance, vast, hunched and amorphous, smoking incessantly. He was, I thought, like Charles Laughton with a stubbly white beard and moustache. Each man who entered kissed his hand; there was also much whispering in his ear. He was very fat and contrived to be stately with it all, but he blew his nose on to the floor; he also ignored the ashtrays with which the slaves had surrounded him, and threw the stubs still burning on to the reed matting. There was a vast and various spread for dinner, but Mehsin sat apart from us, eating his way steadily and messily through a large and somewhat raw fish.

For all his absurdities he gave the impression of power and shrewdness; well filling his position as one of the great figures of Southern Iraq. Throughout the evening his *wazir*, small, pockmarked, scribish and viperish, sat on the floor near his master with a huge ledger open on his knees, making a seemingly casual entry from time to time. Mehsin talked with Thesiger with increasing animation; after a while I could follow little or nothing of what they were saying. Their intensity gave me the impression that they discussed momentous matters. Suddenly Thesiger seemed at a loss, and turned to me. "What was the date of Ethelred the

Unready?" Even had I been less taken aback I should not have found the answer. After a few minutes there was another pause, and Thesiger said "Gavin, I'm very bad at knowing this sort of thing—how long is St. James's Park?" Finally, "What word would we use in English for someone who lies in bed all the morning?" "Slugabed," I hazarded, and Mehsin sent his *wazir* over to me to copy it down into his ledger. "Slukabeed," they repeated over and over again with evident satisfaction, and later it became in this form a much-used term of opprobrium among our canoe boys.

Mehsin's son Ali has little of the presence of the old man; his face is loose, cruel, and self-indulgent, and he has a sadistic sense of mischief. Once when Thesiger told one of his canoe boys to tie up the *tarada* near the stone fort Ali gave orders for the boy to be beaten up and thrown into the river. He also possesses a box filled with spikes, in which those who incur his displeasure are placed and shaken up.

Ali boasted a *sarifa* besides a *mudhif*, and it was in the *sarifa* that we slept that night, on beds carried in from the fort. I revelled in the guilty pleasures first of sitting in an arm-chair and then of sleeping on a mattress, but less in the third western amenity that so many sheikhs boast—the unspeakable lavatories.

Away from the towns practically no one except a sheikh would think of possessing such a thing anyway. In the marshes one takes a canoe into the reed-beds and perches precariously on its wobbling side; on the dry land one merely walks a little distance from the houses. (If one has a servant one says to him *harid ibrig*, "I want to wash"—a curiously European euphemism—and he leads the way carrying a jug of water.)

A number of the sheikhs' forts, however, possess lavatories whose function must surely be that of prestige rather than convenience. These are usually on a river bank, four stakes round which a screen of reed matting is stretched over a shallow trench cut into the mud. The trenches are presumably intended to be sluiced down into the river, but I never saw one that had been within a recent past. In dry sunny weather a million flies form a cloud like a solid obstacle; in wet weather the scene is better left to the imagination.

Coffee pots

Chapter Six

THE next morning we made a short journey to the village of Sahain. On the way we passed long processions of water buffalo being towed by canoes heading northward towards Naija, the swimming beasts urged on by quick loud cries like the honking of wild geese. The great hailstorm had been responsible for consequences more serious than prolonged failure to rebuild the tottering *mudhif*; it had destroyed the reed crop that is the marshmen's livelihood, and many of them, reduced below the level of subsistence, were forced to sell their buffaloes in the market at Naija.

Sahain turned out to be a big huddle of islanded houses criss-crossed by big and small waterways, running at right angles to each other like streets. In the centre of the village stood a small stone fortress, rushed up by Dakhil four years ago, when insurrection by the community against his father Mehsin had seemed imminent. The fortress was still garrisoned, and the muzzles of light machine-guns poked from its loopholes with a glint of dark metal. Just such another village had not long ago rebelled against their sheikh, and when the villagers had overcome his garrison the government had confirmed their independent status. It is easy to see how what may be for the state the only sensible solution to one problem may create a precedent forming others.

In this war-like setting it was a surprise to find that here was the first village that we had visited whose children went to school, and therefore spoke—though did not understand—a few sentences of English. English is compulsory at all Iraqi schools, and is taught by the Direct Method, of which Desmond Stewart and John Haylock have given an illuminating description in *The New Babylon*. They learn, as I was to discover later, after some perspiring hours with their teachers, from Iraqi English Masters who are incapable of carrying on the very simplest conversation in any language but their own, but who have a few parrot-learned phrases and are able to read aloud with just-recognisable pronunciation from children's primers.

I was sent out that afternoon to perform my now customary but still precarious function of shooting coots or duck for the evening meal, and the boy who paddled my canoe was determined to exercise his English; probably he wanted to score off his schoolmaster by retailing the grammar or pronunciation of a real Englishman. It was amazing how much he really could say when he tried, but much more amazing how little he could understand; nothing, in fact, but single words, and then only after constant repetition.

"In English please what is this?" He indicated the boat. "You have not answer my question. Is 'motor-water'?"

A little later, after the inevitable disgrace, "Now Sahib Thesiger will not be your friend any more, because he very much love cartridges." Then, with a hint of avarice "Does Sahib Thesiger love *empty* cartridges too?" Reassured on this point he began again. "Why are Iraqis yellow men and English red men? Answer my question. You have not answer my question; please answer my question. Why I yellow you red?" He wasn't, in fact, very yellow, but as time passed I began to grow red.

At last I did shoot a duck, and as he held the carcase with its head pointing toward Mecca and began to slit its throat he asked "At England which way you point?" and then, impatiently: "Muslims, *this* way, head blood to *Mecca*—at England *how*?" I remembered how in Morocco I had been speaking to an Arab when a water-seller passed with his sheep-skin of water and his tinkling brass cups that cost a penny to drink from: "How much do water-sellers charge in London?" the Arab had asked.

At Sahain that night I saw professional dancers for the first time, a man and his fourteen year old son. Our host brought them in to dance for us after we had eaten, but the boy sat down as soon as he had made his greetings, and no amount of cajoling could make him dance one step. His shoulder-length hair had been shaved two days before because he was going to school, and he wore a red skull-cap which he fingered nervously as he sat cross-legged and stared at the floor. At last he consented to drum while his father danced, and there were tears in his eyes as he watched the man tie his headcloth to resemble swinging hair, two dangling ropes of cloth with a heavy knot tied at the bottom of each.

The father danced well, and the erotic passage brought the usual applause from the audience, but I could not take my eyes from the boy. As he drummed he looked only at the rhythmically swinging *keffia* that was doing duty for his own lost hair, and slow tears rolled unnoticed down his face. His hands on the drum worked in a frenzy as though they had some life independent of himself, as though they were controlled by the rhythm of his father's flying feet rather than by his own sad head shorn of its pride. The drums of stretched pelican-pouch have a twang like the plucked strings of a stringed instrument; they can be plaintive and melancholy, or menacing and ferocious when struck, as they were now, in quick hard rhythm. So furious was the fluttering of his hands on the drum that they left a succession of different positions on the retina of the eye, from the open upraised palm to the flat back of the hand as it struck. Never once did he turn his eyes from the swinging knots at his father's head, until suddenly the drum split under his hands, and as he bent over it I saw him wipe his face quickly with the skirt of his *dish-dasha*. Pity Samson at the mill with slaves.

During the talk round the fireside that night I heard mentioned again and again the name Ghadbhban, and after a while I asked Thesiger who this man might be. "A bandit," he replied, "although actually rather more than a bandit; it's a strange story."

At the end of the First World War Ghadbhban, of the family of Beni Asad or Sons of the Lion, had refused submission to the British and had built himself a fortified position on one of the mud islands in the marshes. The first attacks against him were unsuccessful, and at length the British, with the aid of a powerful Arab, prepared for him a ruse. They sent a bombing aircraft, while the Arab ambushed Ghadbhban's retreat from the island, and into this trap he fell. His canoe and gear were sunk, and he himself severely wounded in the leg. He escaped through the reeds, carrying his child, and sought refuge among the pastoral tribes of the uplands near to the Persian frontier.

Some thirty years later, in 1954, Ghadbhban's brother Faleh decided to try whether he could not play the same hand with greater success. He occupied the same island that his brother had so ignominiously vacated, and levied and looted from the surrounding territory until at last the government recognised his claims and granted him land. During the time of his thrall rumour had gone round the marshes that he had attempted to hold up Thesiger's party, and that there had been a battle. Thesiger himself was said to have escaped after inflicting damage upon Faleh's men, but it was understood that Amara and Sabeti had been killed, and they arrived at their home village to find their parents preparing to mourn their deaths.

Away among the shepherd tribes to the east, Ghadbhban, who had spent his life in exile from the land that he regarded as his own, heard of his brother's doings and of the final successful negotiations with the government. What Faleh could do, it must have seemed to him, he could do too, so back he came to the island that had by now played so large a part in his family history, and with an armed band he was now following his brother's example of loot and levy. Only last week, we were told, he had successfully held up a large cargo boat coming up the Euphrates with a cargo of dates and rifles.

I thought again of the insoluble problems of this intelligent and benign government; of how quickly the diplomatic handling of one problem could lead to another.

When we left Sahain we were right outside the marshes, in a land of semi-inundated rice fields, where every islanded strip of mud was thronged with a multitude of birds: storks, herons, egrets and great flocks of wading birds. Among them stood the ubiquitous eagles, strangely ignored by the press around them, as though they were indeed the purely heraldic symbols that their stylised attitudes suggested.

We came in the late morning to Umm el Gaida, a large village of Sayids on both banks of a wide channel. With these people Thesiger had had little contact in the past, finding them aloof and inclined to distrust the presence of an unbeliever, but our treatment was very different now. His reputation had spread year by year, and by now it had reached here, for from both banks Sayids called to us to come and eat with them.

Throughout our journey I was struck by the boorishness of western hospitality by contrast with that of the Arabs. If a stranger rings a doorbell in Europe, he must produce some very good reason before he can get into the house at all, much less eat there as a guest; yet in the lands where there are neither doors nor doorbells the stranger is not asked the reason for his presence, and to hesitate in setting food before him would be shameful. In the parable of the Good Samaritan it is possible that the significance of the travellers passing by on the other side has been missed; it had to be on the other side that they passed, as though quite unaware of the thieves' victim, because had they acknowledged the other's presence at all there would have been no alternative to the actions of the Samaritan.

Both the European's boorishness and the Arab's profligate hospitality may be no more than separate manifestations of the will to power, but the first must mean security only for the individual, the second for the race.

We stopped at the *mudhif* of an important Sayid, and even a spectacled white-turbaned priest from Naija treated us with courtesy, and did not, as did most of those whom we met later, leave the building as soon as we had entered it.

The meal was lavish; a boy who went to school in Amara dismembered the chicken in front of me. "Here," he said as he handed me a morsel, "I am eating you." "Feeding me, you mean," I said. His fingers worked busily in the gravy-covered carcase. "Yes," he repeated in happy preoccupation, "I am eating you. I eat you very large." Like the boy at Sahain he understood no word of the language he was speaking.

We had intended to leave the village that afternoon, but we had gone little more than a quarter of a mile upstream, the houses still on each side of us, when another Sayid called to us from the bank to come and drink tea with him. Thesiger declined at first, saying that we were expected far ahead by nightfall, but he was so insistent that we ended not only by drinking tea but by staying the night with him. He was so extravagantly polite that it struck me that he must want something from us, but, Arab fashion, it was some time before the request emerged. I was beginning to understand a little of the language now, and could often follow the gist of a conversation provided that it developed along orderly lines. After the formal greetings and a little small talk he asked Thesiger about his doctoring, and whether he was carrying medicines with him; then he added that there were some people here who would be grateful for his attention.

In due course these prospective patients appeared, a group of a dozen or so boys who held their *dish-dashas* awkwardly away from their bodies. This was my first sight of the appalling effects of native surgery, and what I saw made me feel that Thesiger fully deserved his position of minor deity among the marsh peoples. These boys had been circumcised no less than three months before by a wandering professional, and the results were sickening. The magic powder had done its work, producing degrees of inflammation and sepsis so great that it seemed impossible that they could ever heal. Our host produced these unfortunate children by way of persuasion, for he wanted his own son circumcised, and was unwilling to entrust him to the perpetrator of these surgical outrages.

The appeal, made by a Sayid to an unbeliever, was the highest possible mark of confidence and acceptance; as a gesture, however, I saw it rivalled later during our journey, when one of the professionals themselves, a little shamefaced, brought his son to us with the same request.

This was the first community of Sayids that I had visited, and since previously I had only seen them singly and away from their kind, receiving from the common people the exaggerated deference due to their status—(everyone rises when a Sayid enters a house, and no man should ever precede him or otherwise turn his back upon him)—it was something of a shock to realise that they were after all part of a strictly secular hierarchy, descendants of a man who had never claimed divinity. Thus it was with a sensation of anomaly that as we sat round the fire that evening I noticed the number of pistol holsters visible as bulges or edges beneath the garments of our host and our fellow guests; the same sensation as I remember when I saw photographs of the fabled, stately figure of the Glaoui drawing an automatic against his assailants in Morocco; almost as if the Pope were to open fire with a sub-machine-gun upon a group of Protestant heretics.

For some days we pottered about the cultivating lands and the outskirts of the marshes. We stayed sometimes in primitive reed dwellings whose floors, littered with straw and buffalo dung, were transformed in a space of minutes after our arrival by the laying of many carpets and cushions; sometimes in sheikhs' *mudhifs* or forts. One of these, I remember, was pockmarked with bullet-holes and chipped masonry; it had withstood some ten years before a lengthy siege from Mehsin's men, who came on in waves and at last retired leaving sixty dead before its walls.

But it is nights in the reed houses, whether in the marshes or on the banks of the waterways, that I shall always remember best; and, with all their discomforts, the image they bring is one of nostalgia. I remember the pain of massage and its intolerable prolongation, and I remember nights that were hopping with fleas, but I remember, too, the proud curving silhouettes of the canoes and their reflections on moon-whitened water, the moon gliding through troubled cloud and the village women wailing for the dead; the fresh wind blowing through the house all night with the smell of rain upon it; the night sounds and sweet breath of the buffaloes at the end of the house. I used to wake in the night and take in these sights and sounds with a curious intimacy, like memories of childhood, as though they were things once known and forgotten.

At Hadam, a huge reed village standing in newly-flooded seasonal marsh, we were told that the surrounding country was swarming with wild pig, and that a child from a neighbouring village had been severely gored the week before. Here I had my first experience of a different kind of pig hunting.

Some half a mile from the village rose a low tumulus island, whose highest point, where it ran up from sloping banks to a small cairn of turf, was some thirty feet above the water. At the foot of this we drew up the *tarada*, and as we walked up the slope I saw that this had been a burial island, for through the grey-brown dried mud showed everywhere pieces of broken ochre-coloured sherd, bright wedges and chips of green and blue glazed pottery, and loose human bones. On the cairn at the top a dark eagle stood motionless until we were within twenty yards of him.

From the summit of the island we searched the seemingly dead landscape with field-glasses. On every side the water stretched away to the horizon, broken here and there by spits of still-dry mud, scattered bulrush stubble, and an occasional dense reed-bed. It was a landscape in two colours, the pale diffident blue of sky and water broken only by the drab of mud-reach and reed. It was strange how empty and lifeless this composition appeared to the naked eye, and how teeming it became through the lenses. Wherever there was a spit of dry ground hordes of small wading birds scurried hither and thither; some of the apparent islands revealed themselves as rafts of densely-packed sleeping duck; a particularly opaque reed-bed was recreated as an immobile battalion of purple herons; and a small mud hump a quarter of a mile away showed itself suddenly as the enemy—a sleeping wild boar.

This was the first opportunity I had had to examine one of the wild pigs at leisure; and the bulk, compared with the insignificant creatures that I remembered from Kiplingesque pictures of subalterns pig-sticking in India, or from Teuton steel engravings of a fur-collared Kaiser Wilhelm drawing bead upon a pig as it scuttled across a woodland ride, seemed no less than grotesque. This beast was as big, in round terms, as a donkey, but infinitely more solid and massive. There was none of the sparse bristly hair that one associates with a pig; this animal was as shaggy as the shaggiest of dogs, long matted hair of a pale-mud colour, showing dark streaks and patches where it divided between the tangles. He looked eminently able to kill a man.

We walked down the slope of the island and began to wade towards him, for the depth was not continuous enough to give passage to the *tarada*. The water was numbingly cold, not much more than ankle deep, but below it one's feet sank into another four or five inches of stiff sucking mud. After twenty yards I had discarded my shoes, which had been chosen to slip off easily when entering a house, and after fifty I was at least that distance behind Thesiger and Amara. It was not only that the legs of my trousers would not stay rolled up—the others had only to hitch up their *dish-dashas* round their waists—but as soon as I had removed my shoes I had found that the invisible mud bristled with a spiny stubble of burnt reeds as sharp as porcupine quills. It was like walking over a fakir's bed of nails. Every two or three yards one of my feet would slip into the deep prints of an animal or human who had gone this way before, and as I staggered to recover my balance the other sole would come down firmly and with my full weight upon the spikes. I dropped farther and farther behind, while Thesiger and Amara, the former in rubber commando boots and the latter with the horny and insensitive soles of a lifetime barefoot, strode on as unfalteringly as if they walked on smooth dry land.

They were within a hundred and twenty yards of the boar—though I was still double that distance—before he got to his feet, stared truculently, walked a pace or two away, and turned to stare again. Thesiger planted his long fork-topped stick in the mud, rested his rifle upon it, and took aim.

At last I was comforted for my disgrace among the coots.

Thesiger, who is an excellent shot, and Amara, whom he had taught and who was also capable of an impressive performance, each missed the boar three times. The seventh shot struck him in the ribs but did not bring him down nor noticeably slow his progress. We watched him as, far beyond reasonable rifle shot, he trotted on and on through the shallow water until at length he disappeared into the thicket of a reed-bed fully half a mile away.

We followed him. For another half an hour I struggled with the suck of the clay, the slide into indented footprints, the needles of the spiny reed stubble; then, as we neared the tall reeds, the water became thigh-deep and the mud below it softer still. Thesiger halted for a conference with Amara, and I was able to gain a little ground.

Here, where the reeds were in places thick enough to hide a wounded boar, were the typical circumstances for a charge. We floundered forward warily, weapons at the ready, but as I surveyed the party from my ignominious position at its rear I felt that in the event of the pig breaking cover our greatest danger would not be from the pig but from each other. Amara had separated from Thesiger and was now wading at right angles to his course, his rifle horizontal and pointing straight at me, while Hassan, who from solicitude had maintained a mid-way station between them and me, zigzagged about brandishing a Colt .45 automatic whose muzzle menaced each of us in turn.

The boar, however, was not in the reed-bed, and when we emerged at the other side he was standing broadside in shallow water a hundred yards away. Thesiger and Amara fired simultaneously, and this time he died as big game should, shot cleanly through the heart.

This was the only boar, of the many that we killed, of which I had a chance to take a single measurement. He lay dead in water a few inches deep, and I stretched a tape-measure from one of the fore hooves while Amara held it taut at the shoulder. The height was forty-three inches, and though he was old and his tusks were ingrown, curling into the flesh below his eyes, he was, I am certain, smaller than many that we saw and some that we killed. Smaller than the boar that later came very near to killing me.

Near Hadam we met with the first open hostility from a member of a sheikh's family. The sheikh himself, though he was polite enough, was unprepossessing, a little like Mehsin stripped of his dignity. His son was an aggressive young man who wore a gigantic solitaire diamond ring, and who looked to me from the beginning as if he intended to make his presence felt in some way.

When we had eaten, the villagers began to crowd to the fort to be doctored by Thesiger. He had been working for perhaps half an hour, on the hard ground surrounding its walls. He was treating a girl of about fourteen when the sheikh's son came hurrying from the fort, crying to the people to disperse, and to Thesiger that it was an unspeakable shame for him to doctor a girl of their people. He used the worst of all words for shame. Thesiger was naturally angry; the drugs that he used cost a great deal of money, he risked infection himself, and he worked hard for the people. The sheikh himself followed his son and intervened, telling Thesiger to pay no attention and to treat anyone he would, but the atmosphere was unpleasant and ambiguous. Thesiger closed his medicine chests and we retired to the shabby darkness of the fort's reception room. Neither the sheikh nor his son followed us, but after some minutes an ambassador appeared in the form of a negro retainer begging us to examine his entirely healthy child.

Though the incident was not serious it was a reminder to me of the Muslim attitude towards women. By the stranger the women are simply ignored; they should neither be inquired after, nor greeted, nor looked at. The taboo extends to asking after a man's family, because this automatically includes his womenfolk. In Iraq the women are not veiled, but among the primitive people they will very seldom allow themselves to be photographed, and they keep so alert an eye upon the camera that it is almost impossible to take them unaware. The young girls are often vividly beautiful, with the enormous liquid eyes that have been so often compared to those of a gazelle, a delicate golden skin, and hair that—when it has not been dyed with henna and twisted into an ugly elaboration of many short plaits—is usually arranged in a short fringe over the forehead, fine, blue-black, and gently waving; but at some time during adolescence the complexion often becomes disfigured by one or more scars from the disease known as Baghdad boil. At about the same time, too, their faces are tattooed, not elaborately, but enough to impair a beauty dependent upon purity and simplicity. The tattooing does not vary much and is always the colour of blue-black ink; almost always it involves the eyebrows, sometimes as a line parallel to but above their own, sometimes following a line from which the hair has been plucked. The lines of the tattooing are always straight, destroying for ever the tender and moving planes of young frontal bones and temples; a thick line drawn downward from the centre of the lower lip over the point of the chin imposes a further impression of rigidity. This line sometimes extends down over the throat and between the breasts, with right-angle extensions outward over the torso, each line ramified by small projections like the teeth of a garden rake. I glimpsed this once or twice through a momentary accidental exposure, and I do not know how far down the body the tattooing customarily extends. The hands and wrists always carry the same rake-like pattern of straight lines, and often the palms and finger-nails are dyed with henna. Though a woman's everyday working clothes are black as a crow—the *abba* that corresponds to the man's *dish-dasha*, and differs little from it except in the round collar line and the greater mass of material—

girls and young women often wear the gaudiest possible colours, vermilion, electric blue or multi-coloured floral designs. If the cut of the garments were more pretentious they would seem garish and shoddy, but the extreme simplicity of the straight falling lines flatters these cheap imported materials from India and Japan. Young girls have no headcloth; they simply wear the outer black cloak draped from the head rather than the shoulders and from under it they look sideways at a strange man with a doe-like allure and mistrust, but older women wind what appear to be several black cloths round their heads, an unidentifiable mass that gives a bulky effect like a big turban, and extends down the sides of the face and under the chin. Loose ends of this cloth hang to breast level, and often contain charms and other odds and ends knotted into them.

Women often carry enormous loads of decoration in precious metals or semi-precious stones, ear-rings of silver or turquoise, sometimes a heavy silver nose-ring in one nostril only, multiple bracelets, finger rings, and anklets. Whereas a man or a boy wears rings only on his right hand, women display them on both. Perhaps the strangest adornments are the heavy anklets of bright raw silver apparently shaped on *in situ* as a permanency, and appearing so bulky that it would seem impossible for the wearer to walk without acute discomfort. They are of the shape of a cylindrical horse-shoe, open and turned slightly outward at the Achilles' heel, but the aperture is little more than an inch wide, and though I speculated much about it I came to the conclusion that they could not be removed without cutting through the metal.

The girls marry young, rarely later than seventeen and often several years earlier. They come virgin to their marriage beds, for the penalty for detected intercourse before that is no less than death; her brothers will cut her throat. The seducer, on the other hand, is held to be guiltless. It is through the womenfolk of his household that a man can be brought the deepest shame in the eyes of his world, and he exacts for it the full penalty, without mercy and without compromise. If the killer be brought to justice the crime is treated with leniency; as in other cases of ritual murder among the tribesmen, he receives a sentence of three years' imprisonment instead of the normal fifteen.

There are said to be a few, but only a very few, prostitutes in the area, and for the most part these are probably in the places of pilgrimage outside the permanent marsh. It would appear that a prostitute could only begin her profession as the daughter of another, or as a fatherless child whose brothers would for material reason connive in her shame.

Parents arrange the marriages of their children, and though in the marshes it is quite likely that the bridegroom will know his prospective wife by sight, there is no theoretical reason why he should. He will, except in unusual circumstances, be of the same tribe, and he or his father will have paid the bride price of 75 dinar (about £75) or three buffaloes. (The fact that a blood feud can be settled, other things being equal, by the payment of seven women, suggests that a man's life is valued at about £500.)

Muslims are allowed by their religion to have four wives at any one time, and unlimited concubines; divorce, furthermore, is dependent only upon a payment by the husband, who need give no reason for his action. The Prophet's grandson Hassan had set an early example in this respect; he had run through no less than a hundred wives when, at the age of forty-one, a member of the current quartet murdered him.

Most of the marshmen, however, are unable for strictly economic reasons to embrace either these privileges or the risks inherent in them; they rarely have more than two wives, often only one, and no concubines. Quite a different situation obtains among the wealthy landowning sheikhs. Two days journey back from Hadam we had stayed at the fort of a sheikh who was away visiting a relation; we were greeted by his son, a fat smooth-faced boy of fifteen who already had three wives.

Thesiger has described the marriage ceremony—or more properly celebration, for in the marshes it is a social rather than a religious function—in one of his published works.*

"A marriage among the Ma'dan is always an occasion for great festivity. If the bride belongs to another village the bridegroom's friends set out in the morning in their canoes to fetch her. The bridegroom never accompanies them but remains behind in his house. The greater part of the day is spent at the bride's village in feasting and dancing. Towards evening everyone collects at the bride's home where they dance the *hausa*, or war dance. One man sings a couple of lines, which the others then repeat in chorus as they stamp round in a circle, brandishing their weapons and firing off their rifles. The bride is then placed in a canoe and is taken to her new village, accompanied by a great crowd in canoes, singing and firing off shots. The party, known as *zuafif*, stops at any village through which it passes, and lands at one or more of the houses to dance the *hausa*. The rejoicing reaches its climax as they approach the bridegroom's home. I recently attended the wedding of an orphaned boy called Dakhil. He had disposed of almost everything which he possessed in order to pay the bride price, and had not even a hut of his own. He had erected a small red mosquito net as his bridal chamber at the end of his cousin's house, which he had spent the greater part of the day in lengthening. Since he belonged to a different tribe from the rest of the village, it seemed likely that his marriage would be a small affair, but as he was an old friend of mine I turned up with a party and we fired off a considerable number of shots while we fetched his bride. This firing attracted the marshmen from the surrounding villages and his marriage became, for this village at any rate, the event of the year. In the evening the house was packed to suffocation and many people had

* *Journal of the Royal Central Asian Society*, January 1954.

to sit in their canoes outside, while inside the singing and dancing was continuous. At midnight I left, thinking that Dakhil would be glad if the party broke up. When I saw him in the morning he was without his headrope and his new shirt was sadly torn. His friends, who had remained behind in the house, laughingly maintained that when he went to his wife she had thrown him out into the water, a charge which he indignantly denied. With these Arabs it is customary for a man to fire off a rifle as soon as he has consummated his marriage. Dakhil certainly fired off a shot."

Inside a marshman's own home his woman may exert a profound and lively influence, and there is very much more comradeship between them and their husband or father than their total segregation outside the family circle would suggest. The men and women of a household habitually eat together when no outsider is present, and the women will sit and drink tea with guests whom they know very well, but they may never eat with strangers. They have a strict position in the family, a role not absolutely menial but outside which they may not step. If a Ma'dan community were transferred without conditioning to a European city it is, for example, the women who would rise to offer their seats in public transport to their menfolk, who must always be honoured both in word and in deed. Travelling in a canoe with his family a man will take the place of honour and squat smoking in idleness while the women paddle or pole, for it would be unseemly for him to work as one of them.

In the same way tradition relegates to the women all tasks that are considered unmanly; no man will ever draw water if a woman is present, and no man will in any circumstances gather buffalo dung or pound grain. This last is so individual a task, and its performance partakes so much of ritual, that it is difficult to imagine it done by men, or indeed in any other way than became so familiar to me after even a short time in the marshlands. Two women place the grain that is to be pounded in a container that is always the same, a two-foot length of hollowed-out palm trunk that stands upright like a narrow tub. Each takes the haft end of a mallet used for pounding reeds before mat-making, and strikes downward into the tub in alternative rhythm with the other; at the same moment as the thud of impact she gives vent to a grunting cry in a different key to her companion. The sounds are like those made by a tennis ball struck hard with a racquet; when the grain pounders are out of sight it would be easy to believe that one was listening to a new ball game played with two racquets of steel strings, one with a high twang and the other with a low. They would be inconvenient sounds for a man to have to make.

Whether it be from hard work or from frequent child-bearing or from the prevalence of disease, the women of the marsh Arabs become old very quickly. They are in their flower in their early teens, and ten or fifteen years later they seem already middle-aged. One must presume the infant mortality to be enormous, for neither sex employs any method of contraception, yet families even of southern Mediterranean size are rare. By reason of her early age, every girl has nearly the whole of her childbearing life before her when she marries, and even allowing for the phenomenon of adolescent sterility one would expect that a man with two wives would in his old age have at least fifteen or twenty children, but something well under ten would probably be nearer to the truth. For many centuries the balance of nature has been but little disturbed, and the diseases that erase new life amid a storm of wailing from the women have been surer safeguards against overpopulation than the contraceptives of the western world.

Chapter Seven

WHEN we left Hadam we were still going northwards, and away from the marshlands. We moved at first through partially flooded rice fields, and the only navigable parts of them were the narrow irrigation channels, high-banked with loose clay, and so twisting that it was often impossible for the great length of the *tarada* to negotiate their acute bends. We walked balanced on these banks; to me it felt a strange unpractised gait, as if an uncertainly toddling baby were to attempt a tight-rope. Like the alleys of a dream town, the water paths led always obliquely away from the direction of our destination, so that again and again we had to manhandle and lift the loaded *tarada* over mud dams into channels at right angles to our former course. Waist deep in the brown water the canoe boys would heave and strain until the whole length of the *tarada* stood poised upon the centre point of a mud ridge; she would sway there like a see-saw until a final effort set the great scimitar prow dipping to the new channel with a smooth rush like a ship launched down a slipway.

Presently the banks of the winding waterways became lower, and the floods beyond them more and more continuous, until at last they died away altogether, submerged beneath a vast pallid sheet of water that lay before us. An horizon line of a hair's breadth separated the sky from the still water, so that every solid thing inside this great shimmering bubble appeared lapidary, sharply out of key, harder and blacker than ever a black line on white paper could be. Far away on the sunward side, where the sky met the water, a scattered fleet of high-prowed canoes formed etched silhouettes of infinite delicacy. Overhead, long strands of silver cobwebs floated everywhere on the empty blue air;

many carrying a fragment of bulrush fluff that lit them, white-tufted, as they travelled in stately procession high over the still water; one long gleaming thread that hung almost stationary far above us seemed to trail from the crescent moon of the same whitened silver.

For more than an hour we paddled over the enamel surface of the great lake. We passed parties of naked *Berbera*, who fish with nets, strange people of whom Thesiger could tell me little or nothing. Like weavers, gardeners, and, to a lesser extent, pedlars, the *Berbera* are, by reason of their occupation, looked down upon as of lower caste, and a Ma'dan will not eat with them nor intermarry with them. This is strange, in that the inferiority of the *Berbera* would appear to lie specifically in their method of fishing; and as this is the only efficient way of taking fish, the superstition has a curious lack of survival value. The ingenuity that the early Ma'dan displayed in the elaborate exploitation of the natural reed growth of the marshes, together with the introduction of water-loving livestock, suggests that the settlers would have been quick, also, to exploit the great possibilities of the fish that throng the marsh waters. No one seems to know how the prejudice arose against catching them in the obvious way; but it seems to have withstood the blandishments of comparative wealth, for the *Berbera* make a much better living than do the Ma'dan.

Under admittedly unusual circumstances they have at least once made sums that are a fortune by any standards. Some six years ago Thesiger saw a group of *Berbera* who, working where the fish were lying in dense shoals due to freak water conditions, had for at least a week been taking in more than £1,000 daily. The *Berbera* were hiring the Ma'dan to pole the vast boatloads, totalling some forty tons every day, to the nearest point from which lorries could drive the catch to Baghdad.

There are some settled *Berbera* communities, but more often the families or groups are semi-nomadic, moving where generations of experience have taught them that the rise or fall in water level will congregate the fish.

At the far side of the great sheet of flood water the earth dykes began to appear again above the surface, and soon we were once more among the patchy water and irrigation ditches of the rice fields, and once more heaving and hoisting at the unrelenting length of the *tarada*. But as we progressed from channel to channel they became steadily wider and more orderly, and one of them led abruptly into a broad river flowing southwards from the Tigris. Here the dense reed village of Suq ed Tuel clustered both palm-fringed banks; a village of a different type from any that I had seen, for there were busy *suqs* right along the banks, and throngs of people about their everyday affairs. The whole place was as active as an ant-hill, and the narrow path between the shops and the flowing water was like the street of a county town on market day. On the river big trading boats with carved and painted prows towered above the packed canoes, and among the crowds on the bank were sprinkled here and there clothes as diverse as those in Basra or Baghdad. A schoolmaster strolled in the European suit that is the official dress of all civil servants, talking earnestly with a tribesman whose beard was dyed auburn with henna, a not uncommon device among elderly dandies; a policeman in khaki stood before his reed-built police station, and stepped back from the footpath to give passage to a stately white-turbaned priest. The path was intersected by deep ditches leading to back-waters among the palms, each spanned only by a single palm trunk across which the people streamed without a falter or a downward glance.

We landed at a section of the village devoted to boat-building, threading our way with difficulty through the mass of craft huddled against the bank. We negotiated the stern of a huge dhow of a hundred or more feet, to which two men were fitting a new rudder; one of them was using a big drill operated not by a handle but by an instrument shaped and used like a violin bow. On the bank above, an old man, white-bearded and dressed only in a loin cloth, squatted beside a bubbling mud-trough of black bitumen, below which, tunnelled into the bank, glowed a furnace of reeds. From time to time he would stir the seething surface beside him, thoughtfully and ruminatively, and a big blister would rise and burst with a belch of air. Close by, men were coating upturned canoes with the hot bitumen; but to him, I felt, his cauldron was an end in itself.

In the Sayid's *mudhif* where we slept that night we were guarded from thieves not by the usual armed Africans of the sheikhs, but by a simple booby-trap. After we had lain down to sleep our host propped a bamboo canoe-pole across the entrance about a foot above the ground, and, on the floor where a man who tripped over this obstacle might be expected to fall, placed coffee pots and aluminium saucepans. The only victim of this ruse was Sabeti, who went out in the night to relieve himself. I woke as he got up; he remembered to step over the pole as he left, but was too fuddled with sleep to remember it when he returned. He came down squarely on the ironmongery, and woke nobody.

The sounds to which one woke in the morning in a reed house were usually of dogs barking or fighting close to the thin walls, or of the exuberant quacking of domestic ducks a foot from one's head, or the harsh challenge of a cock to the coming day. That morning it was the chirping of a hundred clamorous sparrows that flitted about the reed arches overhead, their voices seeming magnified to the volume of clashing cymbals. I turned over to face the wall and pulled a blanket over my head to try and shut out their din; as I did so I became aware of a snuffling at the reed matting that separated me from the compound outside. It was no more than inches from my face, and the matting was ragged enough to let in a dapple of daylight. Through this golden lace I saw the head of a gazelle, its great liquid eye peering wonderingly into the darkness of the *mudhif*, one delicate hoof scratching daintily at the lattice. I realised that the simile of gazelle's eyes, so well worn by Persian and Indian poets, was in fact a very exact one, for this eye so close to my own was, in its gentleness, timidity, and lustre, startlingly like those of the young Arab girls.

When we left Suq ed Tuel we went downstream, southward toward the permanent marshes, and I found myself looking forward with a curious intensity to a return to that strange world of lagoons and giant reeds and island houses.

From the main channel of the river we turned into a lesser and then a lesser, and for a time we were among the difficult waterways of the rice fields, but always far off on the southern and eastern horizons lay the long pale wall of the reed-beds. After two hours we came out on to a sheet of water as wide and still as that we had crossed the day before, and at its farther side their ranks stood stately and golden. As we neared them there came to us the voices of the frogs, a confused murmur at first, swelling gradually into the remembered chorus that enclosed us like the walls of a room.

The appearance of the marshes had changed during the short time that we had been away from them, for the growth at this time of the year is rapid, especially in the perimeter of seasonal marsh that depends upon the thaw of mountain snows. Everywhere the green spears of the new growth had thrust up through the brittle gold of the old reeds, and at their feet were aquatic plants that had not been there before. As the eye travelled upward there was first the blue sky-reflecting water, on which lay flat purple leaves like those of a water-lily, then the *terre verte* green of water sorrel, and above these the bright green and gold of the giant reeds themselves, their high tops feathered and plumed like roosters' tails.

Because of the new growth, the marshes seemed more than ever a wilderness without paths. I was amazed anew that throughout all these seasonal changes the Ma'dan can recognise through-way from cul-de-sac, can use a vocabulary that lists by name a score or more different types of waterway, and can even tell by the evidence of a few broken or crushed reeds what build of canoe has passed this way before them, a *tarada* or a *bellam*, or the little flat hunting canoe of a wildfowler.

Among primitive people living always in one landscape and with few belongings, there is, I think, a degree of recognition, a photographic memory, that is quite impossible to civilised man. I saw many examples of this. Once, crossing an open lagoon, Hassan called out that he saw concealed in the reeds not less than a quarter of a mile away a canoe that had been stolen some weeks back from a friend of his. At that range I could just, but only just, make out that it was a canoe; I could not even have told to what type it belonged, but when we reached it Hassan proved to be right. On another occasion we were poling in the dark through a broad mud-banked waterway in the land of seasonal marsh. There was a moon, but it was obscured by heavy cloud, and the banks were only just perceptibly darker than the sky. We had on board with us a passenger, returning from a wedding in another village. Suddenly he gave an exclamation and pointed to some dim hulks that to me were just recognisable, by probability rather than by any visual certainty, as buffaloes. He, on the other hand, had recognised them as his own buffaloes, strayed from his village. We put him ashore to round them up and drive them home, and they were, as he had said, his own. Every man, in fact, claims that he would be able instantly to pick out his own buffaloes among a thousand others of these remarkably anonymous animals; by one inch of the tip of a horn, by a fleeting glimpse of some apparently amorphous part of the body, or by their voices, however distant. I expressed disbelief about this to Thesiger, who relayed what I said to the canoe boys. They were indignant; they said that if they were shown, even casually, one service rifle, they would be able a year later to select it from among ten thousand others of the same make. This, it must be remembered, could not be by memorising in the ordinary way the number stamped upon it, for they cannot read. Whether or not that claim is exaggerated, it is certain that they know every seemingly indistinguishable canoe one from another, and this not only in their own villages but in every community within a wide radius of it.

The sun had set by the time we reached Kidi, a satin sunset of oyster and duck-egg blue, against which trailed long skeins of flighting ibis. In the fading light the water reflected the same colours; in the distance only the reed houses and the crescent shapes of the canoes were dark, and in the foreground the clubhead silhouettes of bulrushes stippled against the sky. Across the water came the sound of high-pitched drums beating the rhythm of the *hausa*, or war dance, that announces not only wars but weddings.

We could scarcely avoid following the progress of that wedding in some detail, though we were not among the guests. Soon after we had landed at one of the first houses of the village, houses that again reminded me vividly of ships at anchor, we heard the sound of shots as the bride was removed from her home. The bridegroom's house was a short way across the water from us, and from the time the bride arrived there the drumming and chanting became ever wilder and more fevered as hour followed hour. Presently some professional dancers who had been entertaining the wedding party came across to dance for us. Their mood seemed fired by the occasion, for the movements were more than ever erotic, and after the dancing came two "variety turns" each of which had as its climax a complete and

unstylised representation of sexual intercourse. It is curious
that these turns are almost always of satire against *haji*
(priests or holy men) or against the customs of the religion
that the Ma'dan profess as a matter of course. The first of
these two was yet another variation upon the well-worn
theme of the rump-in-air position of prayer, which drew as
much applause from the audience as if it were a brand new
joke; the second concerned a *haji* who called repeatedly for
milk, in order to seduce the girl who should bring it. He
was, of course, successful. The part of the girl was played
by a youth who had become engaged that evening, and the
part of the *haji*, very realistically, by one of the professional
entertainers.

By the time they had left us, a little after midnight, the
guests had gone from the bridegroom's house, and the
moonlit village was very quiet. A little later a single shot
signalled the consummation of the marriage; during the
small hours there were three more shots at about hourly
intervals each of them sending every dog in the village into
a frenzy of hysterical barking that took minutes to subside.
I wondered what would have been the effect on the village
of the discharge of a Sten-gun magazine.

Firearms play a large part in the life of Ma'dan tribes, and
few celebrations of any kind are considered complete without the ear-splitting bangs made by guns or rifles in a small
house. Some of the tribes are more heavily armed than
others; the Faraijat seemed to me to have more weapons
than any other tribe we travelled among, but that may have
been only because we spent longer with them. (The tribes
overlap each other, so that a village may contain members
of two or more tribes; Kidi is partly Fartus, who in the main
live farther west, and partly Faraijat. A tribe may be partly
true Ma'dan or marsh dwellers and partly cultivators on the
land outside the marshes, but each is identifiable to another
by accent and use of words.)

The commonest type of weapon in the marshes is the

muzzle-loading shot-gun. They are made locally, and look it; the barrel may be any old piece of metal tubing, and several that I saw had quite plainly been constructed from old iron bedsteads, of which some enterprising pedlar had perhaps carried a load to one of the river towns surrounding the marshes. The crude woodwork is usually attached to the barrel by encircling strips of raw aluminium or brass, and sometimes the owner decorates it by a coin or two nailed into the stock. The ammunition for these perilous-looking weapons can be bought at most of the larger villages outside the permanent marsh, black powder, and flat sheets of lead pellets all joined together, from which one may break off as many or as few as one likes. The pellets are not round, but neither, for that matter, are many of the gun barrels. When the owner is unable to afford the standard ammunition he will load it with any scraps he can get, but metal of any kind is at a premium in the marshes.

By far the most common of the rifles is the British S.M.L.E., called by the marshmen *ghurka*, after the Indian regiment that introduced them during the First World War, and the Persian service rifle, which they call by the name of its Czechoslovakian manufacturer, Brno. During the British occupation after the last war these could be bought for four dinar (about £4) apiece, but now, though most of them are in bad condition, they command upwards of one hundred dinar, and the ammunition for them some ten shillings a round.

With the muzzle-loading shot-guns the marshmen are amazingly proficient; those of them, that is to say, who make a practice of wildfowling and become skilled in it. They do not, of course, shoot birds flying, and the fact that I found it easier to bring down single duck well up in the air than to shoot several swimming coots with one shot never failed to amaze the canoe boys. The Ma'dan wildfowler stalks his quarry, either from a tiny flat boat like a miniature open-decked gun punt, or wading naked and shoulder-deep in water that is often ice-cold. The smallest hunting canoes are propelled not by paddles or poles, but by the occupant's arms as he lies flat, like the action of the beetle that is called "water boatman". There is a half-way house between lying flat in a hunting canoe and wading with a bunch of reeds held to screen the face, for I saw an elaborately constructed and camouflaged gun-rest designed for a man to push in front of him as he swam or waded crouching in the water. This stalking horse was a V with the point towards the quarry and the sides embracing the fowler—two methodically tied bundles of reeds six feet long, with a wedge bound in at the fine end to keep the arms of the V separate and the structure rigid. Every few inches along the two arms were tied upright sprigs of a scrub thorn bush, and at the junction of the arms a forked stick made a permanent rest for the gun muzzle.

Though, because of the unsuitable terrain, little if any netting of duck is done in the marshes, a great number of birds are caught annually in the flood lands that surround them. A man will rent a suitable site from his sheikh, and will pay thirty dinar or more for the privilege of netting there for one season. There in water an inch or two deep he digs a shallow trench, shaped like the outline of a leaf, to conceal the folds of the clap net. He builds a reed hide directly opposite to one end of the net (if he is not directly opposite, the pull cord will not close the net), and baits the area with grain for long enough for it to become an accustomed feeding place. The side of the hide facing the trap has two holes, one for spying and one for the pull rope, and the fowler squats with one eye to the spy hole and his hand on the rope, waiting for the moment at which the birds are thickest in the catching area. The nets are small, no more than eighteen feet long by twelve across at the widest point, but a man may take up to 120 duck, waders, or whatever happens to be inside the net when he pulls. The netters catch geese very much more rarely than duck, but I was told that last year someone had taken thirty at a single pull.

Throughout the rest of Iraq, outside the marshes, the destruction of bird and animal is pursued on a grand and relentless scale. Without taking account of the innumerable shots fired from muzzle-loading weapons, more than a million shot-gun cartridges are imported, and fired, every year. Partly because of a certain parsimony native to the people, and partly because of the enormous numbers and comparative tameness of the migratory wildfowl when they first arrive in the autumn, it is probably safe to say that those million cartridges represent the death of a million birds. It is a favourite sport among the wealthier people to shoot from cars, whose danger birds are slow to recognise even in countries where they are more common. It has become a popular sport, too, to chase the desert gazelles in this way, and there are taxi-drivers in Amara who make a speciality of it; a party will kill some fifty or more gazelles in a day.

It is, in fact, the species that can most easily be hunted by car, such as the black partridge, that show the most obvious decrease; the great hordes of migratory wildfowl seem as yet untouched. Even in the spring, when many of the migrants have gone, the numbers seem fabulous; every dusk is sibilant with the passage of thousands of wings overhead, every dawn sky speckled with long strings of wild duck heading for the broad lagoons where they will sleep through the day.

At Kidi I saw an example of the rough summary justice that replaces the processes of law in the tribal areas. A youth, the son, I think, of a merchant, borrowed from Thesiger a silver propelling pencil. An hour or so later he returned, saying that he had given the pencil to a child to bring back to the house where we were staying, but that this child had dropped it in deep water; and, it being night, the pencil was now irretrievably lost. Our host was the son of the local sheikh's agent, and he carried, as a mark of his status, a cane not unlike the swagger canes familiar in the British Army. Whether or not the merchant's son already had a reputation for dishonesty I do not know, but the cane-bearer immediately suspected him, and accused him, of theft. Thesiger took no part in the situation, and we were both spectators of what followed.

The merchant's son received a blow across the face with the cane, and he screamed. Several men hustled him to the farther half of the house, beyond the partition; and there, judging by the sounds, he was more or less thoroughly beaten up. The sounds were very unpleasant. At the end of it our host extracted five dinar from the wretched youth, and gave these to Thesiger in compensation for his loss. Thesiger accepted, saying that he would give them back when the pencil was returned to him.

An hour later the merchant's son re-entered the house, the weals showing red across his face and the side of his neck. With him he brought the pencil, very slightly damp and lacking its lead; there was little evidence of any kind to show whether or not it had been dropped into the water. Thesiger was handing him back the five dinar when our host intervened; the money, he said, should be forfeited as a fine for the attempted theft. He tapped his swagger cane judicially, but with a certain menace, on the palm of his hand, and the youth cringed, protesting that the money had been held against the return of the pencil, and that it was now rightfully his. Thesiger upheld him, and the incident closed with everyone in possession of his own property.

We ate, before leaving Kidi the next day, with a past member of Thesiger's crew, a young man who had been so quarrelsome that in the end he had been forced to become a nomad. The length of poor Yasin's stay in any community with whom he settled was the time he took to alienate his neighbours; sometimes it was only days, sometimes weeks.

As if to compensate for his precarious status he had built himself the most perfect reed house I had yet entered. The entrance was direct from the water, and the floor on to which we stepped no more than four inches above it. Not a reed was out of place; it had the air of a model made for a museum, that should be inhabited only by plaster figures who could do it no damage. Halfway down the wall swung a suspended cradle of bulrushes, and the pink baby was clothed in the only piece of pure white material that I ever saw in the marshes. The rugs and cushions were not Yasin's; what he had not got he had borrowed for our reception, for he was almost penniless. The warmth of his greeting to Thesiger was pathetic; he kissed his hand, bowing over it in a fusillade of tremulous greeting and worship, and he trembled from head to foot as though he had a fever. He could not escape his reputation, for when some three days later we discovered that part of the *tarada*'s mooring chain was missing, Amara and Sabeti suggested immediately that it was Yasin who had stolen it; not because he wanted it, but in order to throw a suspicion of dishonesty upon them.

From Kidi we made a short journey through open marsh of island and lagoon to Agga, a dense village built on one large island of solid land; round its perimeter there were more houses dotted over the surface of the water; as though the crowd on land had pushed them off and they were now floating. Here there was an epidemic fever with a mottled rash, and Thesiger was at once in demand to visit those whose condition was worst. He would not allow me to expose myself to the unknown infection, and I left him at the door of the first house he entered, where he stood aside to allow stately and leisured exit to a cow buffalo and her string-muzzled calf. He gave me into the hands of a friendly Sayid, who for nearly two hours escorted me through the village. It was a paralysing experience; we were followed at first by a score of onlookers, but after the first half hour the number had grown to more than a hundred, and the crowd swelled all the time, until nearly every man and child who was not sick with the fever was looking at the white man who was looking at their village. I could not speak to the Sayid because I did not know enough of his language, and I could not ignore him nor allow him to see my back because of the deference that was his due. I could not escape, because there was nowhere to escape to; and I felt, also, that I should be wasting an opportunity to see the whole of a marsh village, a thing that I had never been able to do before.

So I swept on through the village like a general at the head of his conquering host, defended in front by boys armed with sticks against the dogs, and despite circumstances so inhibiting to observation I was able to learn a good deal that I had not known before.

In particular I saw for the first time each of the processes of reed mat making, the industry on which the majority of the Ma'dan are dependent both for money and for covering their houses. The first stage, after the cut reeds have been brought home to the villages, is to split each stem with a short curved knife. This is done with extraordinary speed, but, I noticed, an amount of bloodshed unexpected among people so practised. When the reeds are split one spreads them out flat upon the ground and pounds them with a long-handled mallet whose head was, here anyway, a section of palm log some eighteen inches long. The pounding reduces the reeds to flat strips formed of from three to six still connected strands, and they can be stored at this stage, for the pounding prevents them from becoming brittle. A man weaves squatting on the ground with the reeds spread flat before him; the woven mat is shiny and golden, with the effect of a bold herring-bone pattern. It is these mats that trading boats from outside the marshes collect to sell all over Iraq and even far beyond its frontiers; the marshmen receive about tenpence for a sheet eight feet by four. Recently I saw some similar matting in London, and learnt that it sold for £2 a yard.

Besides roofing and flooring the houses, the matting has many other uses. Big trays of it, with upturned edges, are used for drying grain under the sun, and this grain is afterwards stored in round structures like miniature gasometers, the sides formed of reed matting and the top sealed over with buffalo dung that sets hard like cement.

It was the time of day when the water buffaloes were coming home. Most came unattended; but one straggler was ridden, as she swam in across the lagoon with only her face above water, by a child who held one of her horns in each hand and balanced his folded *dish-dasha* on the top of his head. Those buffaloes that arrived before the canoes had returned with their loads of green *hashish* stood groaning in resentful parties round the walls of their owners' houses. Here, as in other villages where there was dry land between the houses, the fragile walls were protected from the bumping of their heavy bodies and the scrape of their horns by a honeycomb of rectangular pits dug right along the foot of the wall. The buffaloes stared at these and groaned anew.

From time to time the Sayid made some attempt to disperse the dense crowd that thronged round us; and at length, sensing, I think, my embarrassment, he led me into a merchant's house and left the disappointed multitude chattering disconsolately outside.

There is a shop in nearly all of the large villages; it differs in no way from any other marsh house except for the small white flag that flies from a single reed above it. Inside, the back of the house is packed with simple commodities; rice, tea, sugar and salt, sometimes a few bales of cheap cloth, and cigarette tobacco and paper. The tobacco is, by European terms, incredibly cheap; even full-size made cigarettes in cardboard packets cost only about fourpence for twenty, and by rolling their own cigarettes the marshmen can smoke the same number for twopence. Smoking is therefore an item which can hardly trouble any man's budget, and the children begin when they are quite small, sometimes as young as four or five. Despite these encouragements few of the Ma'dan seemed to me to be heavier smokers than the average Englishman who begins in his late teens; and who, at the moment of writing, pays more than twenty times as much for the cigarettes he smokes. Because of their cheapness in Iraq it is customary for a host, if he is at all well-to-do, to offer, as a matter of course, a whole packet of cigarettes to each of his guests, in the same way as in Europe a guest is offered a single cigarette from a cigarette case or box. This is at first disconcerting, more especially as in the *mudhif* of a sheikh these packets are themselves pretentious, gilded and overwritten with flowery Arabic letters. As Thesiger's crew smoked very little, and Thesiger not at all, I used often to leave a *mudhif* with a hundred and twenty free cigarettes thus decoratively clothed.

In this merchant's house there was a wireless set, one of the only two that I saw in the marshes. The sound of it filled the little room, and its anachronism was not apparent, for it was wholly beautiful; a noble voice, full and sweet, intoning verses from the Qu'ran. Like Christianity, modern Islam makes full play upon the senses for the ready emotionalism that they can evoke.

At length Thesiger joined me in the merchant's house, full of descriptions of the fever and its symptoms, and the most embarrassing afternoon of my whole journey came to an end.

In the evening a gale blew up, and the night was full of the rattle and slap of wind in the loose reeds of the house-front, the crying of small children and the batter of rain upon the reed roof. The roof leaked, and a thin trickle of water streamed from it on to my face; I thought the floor too

packed with sleeping figures for me to try and change my
position, but after a time of uneasy dozing an indistinct
figure took me by the feet and dragged me, inert, to another
corner. There was some bustle and activity, and I made out
that our host was taking up the reed matting from the floor
to reinforce the roof. A simple life, where one's carpets and
roof tiles are of the same material.

From Agga, completing a northward loop of our course,
we returned to Bumugeraifat. As we went farther into the
heart of the marshes the change in their vegetation became
ever more noticeable, for now we moved through a deep
and enclosing forest of green reeds. Night came with all the
grandeur that I had come to associate with the setting of the
sun in the marshlands. The sky was chrome-yellow at first,
turning hotter and hotter behind the black lattice of the
reed-beds, while to the east their stems were lit to a glaring
orange, and the water was purple below an already bright
full moon. Far up between two scarlet cloud plumes a single
eagle rode the fading wind. As the last of the sun's light
went, the water was dabbled with bright moon-chips and
the stars burned staring and splendid in a sky bare but for
two long streamers of black cloud.

The moon and stars were brilliant overhead when we
reached the village and drew up the *tarada* at the same island
house at which we had stayed a fortnight before. To return
to a known place, amongst so much that was strange and
unfamiliar, seemed in some way a homecoming.

But it was not, in fact, the coming of guests that pre-
occupied the household, for we stepped from the *tarada* into
the circle of an argument that gave every appearance of
having already lasted several hours. The group sitting round
the fire suspended it for long enough to give us civil
greetings; then they were at it again hammer and tongs.

It appeared that someone in the village had, for some
reason that never became apparent, beaten up someone else,
and the village head man was trying to regularise the position

with the culprit. When we entered, these two were discussing—a mild word, in the circumstances—the pros and cons of the situation. Neither would listen to what the other had to say; within seconds it had become what it had obviously been before our arrival, a screaming match. There were lulls. The head man demanded three dinar in compensation for the injuries of the victim, and the accused agreed. "All right, we pay, but we leave tomorrow." So final, so easy. In five minutes it had all broken out again. The question was still unresolved when the party dispersed before supper.

When we had eaten, the Performing Flea danced for us again. He had sat, small and solemn, through the unseemly bickerings of his elders; now it seemed that he made his own wordless comment on the futility of speech. I would not have believed that his dance could have been wilder than before, but it was; it held now all the tension of the angry voices to which he had been listening, the frustration of the man who was obliged to pay for his exhibition of temper, and the triumph of the victim who saw his oppressor pilloried. One half of all humanity, it seemed to me, crouches nursing a tormented pride, while the other clowns and mimes, vicariously disowning a part in that suffering. There was little that the Flea could say by rhythmic movement of his body that he had not said before; but to express his mood he introduced into his dance a new—and to me a terrifying—extemporary variation. As he paused, jerking and twitching, before each member of the group who surrounded him, he would seize the spectator's nose and give an insolent tug of conquest before moving on to the next. The bones of my own nose had not yet set since the humiliating incident of the Father of the Horns, and the least touch upon it was still an exquisite agony. I sat in terror with my hand shielding my face until at last someone whispered to the child the reason for my lack of co-operation. When he next stopped before me he tore my hand

Village scene at Ramla

Canoe prow and water buffalo

The watch dogs of a river-bank house

Amara with a wild boar

Early morning scene as the buffaloes take to the water

Mudhif at sunset

Interior of a *mudhif*

The principal occupation of reed weaving

A small *mudhif* at the northern edge of the marshes

A young Suwaid

from my face; and, while I was preparing for the worst, he planted a warm wet kiss upon my forehead.

Rain had reduced the buffalo platform to a swamp of dung and *hashish*; in the family half of the house three calves lay contentedly beside the fire, smothered in dung from wallowing outside, and the sickly-sweet tang of it and the cleaner smell of their warm breath was on the air all night. Before I lay down to sleep I went out on to the buffalo platform to relieve myself; I picked my way between the ponderous bodies of the buffaloes, their sides and the ground around them slippery with dung. From the water's edge I had a view of the next house and its buffalo platform, lit by the fire that still burned beyond it; a dog climbed on to a sleeping buffalo's back and composed himself for the night. On the back of the neighbouring buffalo stood a hen, pecking industriously, and on the spine of a third a tiny child balanced upon one leg. Overhead there were wild geese calling far up under the stars.

Thesiger left Bumugeraifat the next day in order to negotiate in a neighbouring village the details of Amara's marriage, and Amara and I set off in a borrowed canoe to shoot pig. We each killed two; it was much easier than I had expected. My second, which I shot swimming, so that his head just disappeared below the surface and never rose again, was the largest boar that I ever saw in the marshes.

Thesiger's negotiations were successful, and the evening became a riotous celebration of Amara's engagement. The tempo increased through drumming and singing and the Performing Flea's wild firelit capers to volleys of shots fired through the reed roof. In the midst of this, when the tumult was at its craziest, a huge figure in the shadows beyond the firelight began to struggle through the squatting press, clutching in both hands a great brass-bound muzzle-loading shot-gun. For a moment or two this formidable piece of artillery wavered uncertainly round the heads of the crowd; then with a roar and a sheet of flame and smoke it had gone off through the ceiling. The report was followed by a long shower of broken reeds and debris; then, in a moment of dead silence, a large bat fell with a clang on to the coffee pots.

It was about this time that the Performing Flea, resting a while from his cyclonic activities, came to the end of a cigarette that he was smoking. He tossed the butt in the direction of the hearth, but it fell short, and landed upon the thigh of a merchant named Hussain, far famed for his meanness and pomposity. The Flea watched, fascinated. For some seconds the stub smouldered unnoticed; then, as it burned through the cloth of the *dish-dasha* to the skin, Hussain leapt to his feet with a yell of surprise and pain. He glared fiercely round him; then, fearful of mockery, and seeing that everyone was looking at him, he turned his yell into the opening chorus of a war dance. In an instant the whole crowd was on its feet, stamping out the rhythm of the *hausa*, roaring the wild menacing chant until the whole reed house vibrated with it. The lantern went out, and the fire became trodden under by the stamping feet, and the darkness was punctuated only by the flash of the guns, each followed by a spatter of loose fragments from above.

When it was all over there were a great many holes in the roof, and everyone got rather wet during the night, but Amara's engagement celebrations had been a great success.

Chapter Eight

From Bumugeraifat we went into the sun in the morning, heading for the Eastern Marshes beyond the Tigris.

We slept the first night at Hauta, the first of the nomad villages, whose people herd great droves of buffaloes and move with them according to their seasonal needs. Here the houses were entirely different from those of the settled Ma'dan, for they seemed no more than insignificant appendages to the huge buffalo-shelters, or *sitras*, that projected from them. These, though joined directly and without division to the end of the house of arched columns, were fifty or more feet in length, and built without arches, the reed tops interlocking in a pointed Gothic arch at the midline of the ceiling, their feathered ends drooping down like a long row of fox brushes. The leaves are not stripped from the reeds used for building *sitras*, and they hang as thin pennants, decorative as though by intention, down the whole length of the upper walls. At the end of that great length the sides and roof taper inward and downward to an entrance small enough for the building to give the maximum shelter to its inhabitants, the huge streams of buffaloes that were sloshing or swimming homeward in herds of a hundred or more as we arrived. As spring progresses, and the need for weather protection becomes less, the buffalo shelters are gradually demolished and used for fuel.

For a long time Amara's family had been at blood feud with a family of this village; it had recently been settled by a payment of women, but throughout the evening I thought he seemed jumpy and ill-at-ease.

The food was the most primitive that I had yet encountered, rice and sour milk; and, since there was no partition between the buffalo shelter and the human living quarters, when I lay down to sleep it was with a buffalo at my head, her warm breath stirring my hair. In the night there was a sough of wind in the long dark tunnel, and it began to rain gently; the fine drops fell cool on my face through a gap in the reeds overhead, and I remember waking to see in the small flicker of firelight a woman suckling her child from withered but gourd-shaped breasts.

The fleas in that house were so numerous that I could actually feel them walking over my body in a dozen places at once. By now, since fleas have a peculiar penchant for me, there was little fresh pasture for them; bite touched bite over most of my body, and their great activity must, I think, have been an effort to find a patch where some other of their number had not already dug his knife and fork. They irritated me so much that at length I got out a torch and began the futile task of trying to reduce their numbers. Up till this time I had supposed, since the opportunities for examination were small, that the near-raw condition of my body was due to fleas alone; now I realised that I was also lousy, and that two separate armies were fighting for possession of my skin. After a moment of nausea, I considered this and realised that there was in any case nothing that I could do about it at that moment, and that it had not worried me while I did not know, so I went to sleep again. It was another week before I had the opportunity to wash myself all over, and when I did, the lice disappeared magically and for ever.

There was, however, nothing that I could do to improve the condition of my feet, and they remained an unpleasant sight throughout the whole time that I was in the Marshes. This was because it was the custom to be barefoot in the *tarada*, as if one were in a house; and though the mosquitoes were never very bad there were enough of them to make a considerable impression upon any surface exposed in continuous immobility for several hours of each day. When the mosquitoes are tiresome a Ma'dan will always cover his feet, as he sits cross-legged, with the skirt of his *dish-dasha*, and I used to envy Thesiger, who habitually wore this garment of the people, since he was able to cover his feet either from the cold or from insects with a mere flick of his skirt. This was only one of many ways in which I found European clothes grotesquely unsuited to the life I was leading; after the first few weeks of distressed acrobatics it became plain to me that the *dish-dasha* was the only possible garment to deal adequately with the living conditions. The wardrobe which Thesiger had outlined in London had sounded exiguous; it proved, in the event, to be sufficient in quantity, but had I lived for the rest of my life among the Ma'dan I should never have learned how to make grey flannel trousers a manageable garment for a wearer who must both wade in marshlands and conform to Arab customs. It would have been absurd for me, who had arrived speaking none of the language, to have dressed as one of the people, but had I had to consider no one but myself, I would have exchanged the discomfort for the ridicule.

On the day we left Hauta we had said good-bye to the Central Marshes, those that lie to the west of the Tigris; for early that morning we crossed the great river, and never returned to them. We crossed open water with a line of palms on the horizon, and as we approached them anachronism sprang up to meet us; a motor horn blared from a few hundred yards away, followed by the forgotten sound of rubber tyres squealing on a hard surface. We passed under the main north-south road, and then we were in the Tigris itself, with the soaring blue-green dome of Ezra's Tomb breaking the line of palms at our left. When the palms ended the river ran through a mud-brown land, flat and featureless; a few yards from the bank the road ran parallel, and down it sped a scarlet Cadillac convertible. The car was open, and the driver's *keffia* streamed behind him in the wind; he can have been travelling at little less than a hundred miles an hour, though his father had probably never been faster than a camel or a horse could carry him.

We followed the Tigris upstream for some miles, and presently the road and the twentieth century diverged from it. We met huge rafts of cut reeds, a hundred feet long and a third as wide by ten feet high, that drifted infinitely slowly downstream. They carried two or three men each; they were floating down to Basra, and the journey would take several weeks.

But reminders of the west were with us again when we stopped to eat at a sheikh's fort on the river bank; there was an empty bottle of Gordon's Gin standing among the coffee pots, and one window of the fort had been repaired with a sheet of tin advertising an American oil company.

The fort was the only sign of human habitation within the limits of vision; on the one side the Tigris flowed between brown mud banks, its surface chopped by a cross-current wind blowing from an empty pale-blue sky, and on the other the silvery edge of the low marshes stretched away over the Persian frontier.

We turned out of the Tigris within a few hundred yards of the fort, and at once we were travelling through the beginning of the Eastern Marshes.

Both the Eastern Marshes and their peoples have an entirely different flavour from those to the west of the Tigris, and this difference is compounded of so many small things that at first I found it difficult to analyse. The people are less formal, both in manner and in dress; the black and white *keffia* of the Shi'a becomes rarer the farther east one travels, and becomes replaced by the brown headcloth worn turban-fashion and without *agal*; the European-style jackets so often worn over the *dish-dasha* in the Central Marshes became fewer and finally non-existent. Hospitality tends to be much less lavish; the people surround themselves by less custom, and display their emotions the more freely. Many of the people, particularly among the nomad Faraijat and Suwaid tribesmen, seemed to me to be of a different physical type, many of them strikingly fine featured, not rarely with green or blue eyes, and growing a fair beard and moustache.

The nearness to the frontier produces, perhaps, a little of the ambivalent mentality common to many frontier folk; there are bands throughout the Eastern Marshes whose chief occupation is smuggling and who are frequently involved in armed clashes with the frontier posts. As, after the first few days, we came nearer and nearer to Persia, the canoe boys became progressively more alert for banditry, for it is easy here for a robber to slip across the frontier.

We travelled north-east, coming diagonally closer to it. We had spent the first night at Baidhat el Nuasil, a seasonal settlement of the Shadda tribe, and our second at Abu Laila (which has the evocative meaning of "Father of Night"), a large village of Faraijat nomads. Beyond Abu Laila the water was scarce, and the *tarada* became stuck in endless blind channels of a water-maze. Here most of the reed-beds had been burned; they remained only as blackened patches prickled with the spikes of new growth, alternating with the deep intense blue of the water patches. This ground was alive with birds: flocks of glossy and sacred ibis, egrets, many species of heron, storks, pelicans, and a myriad waders; above them the eagles wheeled on a blue sky with bursting plumes of white cloud. At the end of this burnt land, when we seemed to have turned back from a thousand cul-de-sacs, we came to a few nomad dwellings, houses with giant *sitras* already partially demolished, and at the first of these we stopped.

Our host was small, wizened, and ragged beyond words. He wore a single garment only, a khaki overcoat that looked centuries rather than decades old, held round his waist by a belt of twisted reeds; the coat did not meet, and revealed the fact that he had allowed his body hair to grow freely. About his head he wore, turbanwise, a twisted rag of unrecognisable colour.

It was here at Jeraiwa that I felt again a quality inimical, almost terrifying, in the landscape itself. The wind had begun to rise soon after we arrived; the sun was suddenly obscured, and the colour drained from the world, as bright sea pebbles dry drab and magicless when wave and sun have left them. Round all the pale horizon the wind bowed and ruffled the silvery sedge, mile upon mile with nothing solid but the immediate foreground.

Yet the height of the distant reed-beds was deceptive, for we had journeyed little more than an hour from Jeraiwa before we reached a large permanent village built upon a huddle of mud islands with broad waterways forming streets between them. Turaba; the name itself brings back to me the curious, uncomfortable savour of an incident that I saw there for the first time, an incident that is a commonplace to these people.

The wind had grown stronger during the past hour, and when we landed it was blowing a rustling, gusty gale, whirling reed fragments into the eyes and covering everything with a fine dust from the dry mud of the islands.

Thesiger had sought shelter from this behind the house, where he was doctoring a child who had had his shoulder ripped open by a pig. Our host was with him, and I was glad that there was no necessity to go immediately into the house and be cross-legged once more. I was standing outside, near to the entrance of the house, looking out across the street-like strip of water between us and the buildings opposite.

The happenings of the next minute were, of course, unrelated, but their strangely precise sequence left me with a single dream image that has not disintegrated.

First, from some unseen quarter of the village came the call to prayer, the only time I had ever heard it in the marshlands. The light was just beginning to fail, and it was the time of day when the women go out from the houses to draw water. From the far bank three women, a few paces apart and equidistant from each other, came down carrying the great jars on their heads, and from the bank on which I stood three more went down facing them. All six drew water, standing knee-deep as they did so; each lifted her vessel on to her head, and turned back towards the house from which she had come. They left the water in unison, as though this were something of mystic significance and often rehearsed, and as they did so a great flight of white egrets came surging low over the surface between the houses, like the foam on a single broad wave sweeping forward; they passed swiftly with a soft rustle of snowy wings, and were gone.

Suddenly from the house immediately opposite to me there broke forth a wild pandemonium of shrieks and wails. Two children burst from the doorway and threw themselves on to the narrow strip of ground between the walls and the water, beating at it with their fists and tearing up handfuls of mud and fallen reeds. Men ran out beating their breasts and bellies, striking insanely at the walls of the house, gathering great handfuls of rubbish and dashing it against their heads. Then two women rushed from the house, frantic and screaming; they ran blindly with their arms upraised, and plunged flat into the water. They remained thrashing at it, floundering deeper and deeper until only their heads were above the surface, and screaming all the while. By the time, minutes later, that they had waded ashore, there were wailing boatloads of mourners converging upon the house from all sides, until the space within it had overflowed and those in the canoes could not land; they stood where they were, bowed and beating their breasts in a frenzy of lamentation.

I had witnessed the moment of death of an old man in the house.

Much of this abandoned, hysterical grief is not so much assumed, or acted, by those to whom the death is of no great personal significance, as communicated to them by the close relations in their moment of agony. Once it has been communicated it is felt as something real; and the whole chain of reactions can be set off by chance, as it were, when in fact there is no death to mourn.

I saw an example of this a few days later, when a woman brought to Thesiger a child with some quite trifling ailment. It was a warm day, and the people of the village—a small nomad village where there was as yet little water—were about their everyday affairs all round us. The child squawked while Thesiger was examining it, and without any warning the mother began suddenly to wail and to beat her breasts. Crying out that her child was dying, she seized some buffalo dung and smeared it on her forehead, and then threw herself prostrate on the ground. Some twenty paces away two women were pounding grain; instantly they threw down their mallets and doubled up in an ecstasy of howling grief, and some children, who had been playing near them, all began to cry. Within two minutes every woman in sight was wailing and striking at her body with her hands, and every child was weeping with the slow desolate misery that is the voice of childhood despair, the voice of the abandoned and unloved. By now Thesiger's patient was terrified and wailing too. The situation was completely out of hand. Thesiger shouted to the people that the child was perfectly all right, and spoke fiercely to the mother. She stopped wailing as suddenly as she had begun, and her face was left frozen in an expression that, now that she was motionless and her crying had ceased, might as well have been a grin of laughter as a grimace of grief. When she saw that her child was after all not dying, she began to laugh, and between the set of her face in her previous misery and her present relief there was not the least difference. Within a moment all the adults were back at work, and the children playing, as if there had been no interruption.

In the Eastern Marshes there are a greater number of tumulus islands than to the west of the Tigris. Many of these, though some are as much as twenty feet high, are too small to carry more than one or possibly two houses, and are thus unoccupied; for the Ma'dan are afraid of robbers and bandits,' and prefer to group their houses close enough for mutual support. The whole surface of many of these tumuli is littered with pottery, much of it glazed; with bricks, whose presence is difficult to explain, and with pieces of laval-looking black stone; some have crater-like formations at their summits, equally inexplicable. A number are burying places for the Ma'dan, and these can never be excavated, for no Muslim will tolerate the disturbance of his dead.

From the top of one of these islands the marsh forms the horizon on all sides, and by that season of the year it is green for the most part, streaked with the gold-buff of high reeds tall enough to hide the scattered villages that lie among them.

From Turaba we travelled northwards through this country, heading for Dibin, the largest of all these tumulus islands, on the northern edge of the Eastern Marshes. It was a day's journey, and we ate on the way at the small village of Abu Sukhair, at a curious dwelling with a wren's-nest entrance three feet up its wall, the only one of that type that I saw. At that house I bought two otter skins, from which the entire carcases had, with seeming impossibility, been removed through the mouth, leaving the skins without a single incision. One of these skins, and the live cub that I eventually brought back to England, proved to be of a race new to science.

It was after dusk when we arrived at Dibin, but the western sky was still yellow on the horizon. The silhouettes of the houses were black against it, and the lit fires within them were of the same colour as the sky, mirrored in still water. A black figure came out from a black house and threw up two black hens on to the roof; they strutted there sharp-edged against the afterglow.

The only *mudhif* at Dibin was owned by a woman, a remarkable departure from normal custom. She was the widow of a sheikh's agent, and now in precarious circumstances as a result of the sheikh's dismissal of his employees.

It would have been impossible to live in Iraq even for a few weeks without having already heard much of this sheikh, one Nasr, son of Salman, for his name was a by-word of perfidy and shame.

He was the youngest son of his father, having a number of half-brothers born of Salman's other wives. Nasr's mother acquired vast influence over the old sheikh Salman, and had schemed and plotted for her son to gain all the inheritance that should rightfully be divided among the half-brothers. It was said that she had poisoned one of them, and was suspected of murdering two others who came to his funeral. Finally, she had persuaded Salman to make over all his property to Nasr.

Nasr made full use of the situation. Within a few months he had acquired the reputation of a cruel and despotic tyrant, extortionate and without interest in the welfare of his people. He had made friends among the more undesirable Europeans in Basra and Baghdad; he drank and he gambled and made ever greater demands on those who owed him allegiance; the wake of his speedboats roaring down the rivers swamped the canoes and houses of the villagers who paid for his luxuries.

At length his nephew Talib, son of one of his murdered

half-brothers, could stand no more. Talib was a boy of only sixteen years, but he rallied his tribesmen and declared war on old Salman, his grandfather who had betrayed him and given all to Nasr. On learning of this, Salman wanted to go himself in his *tarada* to reason with him, but his councillors pleaded with him that this would be suicide; Talib, they said, was outraged beyond all reasoning, and would undoubtedly kill his grandfather. Salman compromised; he agreed to send instead a Sayid as ambassador, whose person Talib would feel obliged to respect. This assumption, however, proved wholly erroneous, for when the Sayid approached Talib's fort, waving on a reed his blue *keffia*, a burst of machine-gun fire cut the canoe in two, and the Sayid was fortunate to escape with his life.

From that time onward Nasr's position became ever more perilous. Salman became ill, and his doctor whispered in his ear that Nasr had offered him an assassin's fee of 3,000 dinar to poison his patient. Salman believed him, and instantly sought to rescind every document made in favour of the son whom he now saw in his true light. Nasr fought him through legal channels, a thing considered shameful in the extreme between son and father, and the dispute was raging in Baghdad when we had arrived in Iraq. The policy of the government was still uncertain. Every Ma'dan was partisan in the dispute; very few stood behind Nasr, and those who did were in all probability inspired by terror of reprisals should Nasr emerge the victor. A young wife whom Nasr had divorced took her revenge by composing a song about his wickedness, and this became the season's song-hit, to be heard on the lips of every cultivator, *hashish*-gatherer and buffalo-herd.

We were to be in the thick of this dispute on the following day, but what claimed my attention that first night at Dibin was a remarkable bird. After we had eaten the evening meal I had gone out for a moment, and returned to find my cushion usurped by a creature whose great orange eyes, an

145

alarmingly long way above the cushion, reflected the fire-light. It was, the people told us, a kind of eagle that they had never seen before; it had risen from the reeds in front of some *hashish*-gatherers, who had knocked it down with a canoe pole. It had been stunned, but was quite uninjured. I turned the beam of a torch on to the dim shape, and the bird blinked but did not move. It was one of the most splendid creatures I had ever seen; an eagle owl, without a feather of its gold and black plumage ruffled, and vast eyes of so intense an orange that it seemed as if some fire must burn behind their lenses. His captors had cut the long feathers of the wings, and it would be many months before he could fly again; it was not difficult to guess that once the novelty of this captive king had worn off he would quickly be allowed to starve. To guard against this, I arranged through Thesiger to pay three dinar for the eagle owl if he was still in good condition when we returned to Dibin in two or three weeks' time. The woman of the *mudhif* agreed readily, and asked what she should feed him on. I explained that he ate flesh, and immediately an old man sitting oppo-site to me suggested throwing the *mudhif* cat to the bird; indeed he had grabbed the cat and was about to do so when Thesiger intervened. I remembered that every *mudhif* was alive with bats and sparrows, and at once an enthusiastic crowd began poking and rattling sticks in the dark crannies of the reed arches. The bats escaped easily, shooting through the low door and out into the quiet starlight; sparrows fell, but the cat, unconscious of sentence or reprieve, was on them before ever they touched the ground. I wished, after a while, that the old man had had his way with her, for it was half an hour before we had collected enough to feed the owl.

The next day Nasr's eldest half-brother Jabir arrived at Dibin. How much Salman's rightful heirs had lost became apparent, in that Jabir did not even own a *tarada*. His retinue of some half-dozen men was, however, heavily armed, and his face looked wolfish and purposeful.

He was distrustful of our presence, and did not immediately disclose the purpose of his visit. Presently he mentioned Salman and Nasr, almost casually, testing the ground in front of him. Thesiger said, "I do not know your father, but I have heard nothing but good of him; of Nasr I can only say that I dislike him the more each time I meet him, and that the last time I went to his *mudhif* I came away hungry."

With this lead Jabir began to elucidate the position. He had surrounded Nasr's nearby fort, and sent word to its occupants that anyone who showed his face outside its walls would be killed. As a result, Nasr's fort, which had been progressively strengthened over a number of years, had now, to avoid bloodshed pending the legal decisions in Baghdad, been reinforced by a police contingent.

Jabir was here to canvass the allegiance of these tribesmen who Nasr had usurped from him, so that in the event of a government decision in favour of Nasr they would follow Jabir into war. Old Salman had given four hundred armed men to Nasr at the time when he had made over to him all his property, but three hundred and fifty of these were rumoured to have deserted back to Salman when they had heard the doctor's story of the bribe to poison the old sheikh.

Jabir promised land to those who would fight for his cause, and his retinue distributed ammunition. The trouble, it seemed, was to begin in three days' time.

Thesiger said, "Now we shall have to get out of this district. It's our responsibility to keep clear of internal troubles in the country, no matter where our sympathies may lie. I've never been involved in politics, internal or external, and I'm not going to start now."

But we were in for a noisy afternoon, despite these admirable sentiments.

Jabir sat with his retinue at one side of the coffee hearth.

Presently he called for a cigarette packet to be propped against the inner wall of the *mudhif*, above the entrance some ten yards from him. When this had been arranged to his satisfaction he threw up his rifle, took a long aim, and pulled the trigger. The cigarette packet fell to the ground in a golden shower of reed fragments, followed by a fusillade of applause. A man ran forward to pick it up, and found that it had not been hit. Nettled by this, Jabir had the packet set up again, and his third shot struck squarely in the centre. He invited us to try the same target; we were somewhat farther down the *mudhif* than he, and we had a Colt .45 pistol against his rifle, but both Thesiger and I were fortunate with our first shots. Then a matchbox was substituted for the cigarette packet, and the whole performance started again. At the end of ten minutes a cigarette had taken the place of the matchbox, and the *mudhif* was cloudy with the thin bitter haze of expended cordite. We were consistently lucky; I use the word with no false modesty, for the dimensions of the cigarette were in fact smaller than the grouping capacity of our weapon at that range. There was nothing halfhearted in Jabir's acceptance of the challenge; he went on shooting in rapid fire until he blew a cigarette in half with his twenty-seventh shot.

The stub still remained stuck in the reed pillar, and instantly an elderly Sayid, the chief of Jabir's retinue, grasped his rifle and sprang to his feet. He stood splay-legged, waggling a little, like a golfer addressing his ball, threw up the rifle to his shoulder and fired apparently without taking aim. A little fountain of reed chaff shot out from the pillar no more than an inch to one side of the cigarette. Thesiger got up and walked across to it; he had his finger in the hole the bullet had made, and was in the act of turning back to speak, when I saw the rifle-butt slam into the Sayid's shoulder for a second shot. I yelled to Thesiger to duck, and as he did so the bullet passed six inches over his head and grazed the paper of the cigarette, leaving the tobacco showing. I doubt if Thesiger had been nearer to death or mutilation during his five years in the marshes.

The Sayid ran from the *mudhif* to the hard earth outside the door, and crying, "*With Salman against Nasr!*", he fired his rifle into the air. Jabir followed him, and behind Jabir went everyone in the *mudhif*, jostling to form a circle round him. "*With Salman against Nasr!*", shouted Jabir, and the crowd took up his words in a chant as they began to stamp in the savage rhythm of the war dance. As they danced they swung their rifles round their heads, firing them the while, and the bullets whined away over the empty miles of marsh which were Jabir's rightful heritage. Most of these men, if they went through with what they had begun, would be dead within the week, for without heavy arms the sheikhs' forts are almost impossible to take by storm. But the garrison of Nasr's fort must have trembled, for to them it must have sounded as if the battle had already begun.

"We must go," said Thesiger. "We're here by courtesy of the Iraqi Government; we can't be partisans."

When the *hausa* was over we said good-bye to Jabir, breathless and sweating and with his headrope askew over one eye, and we left.

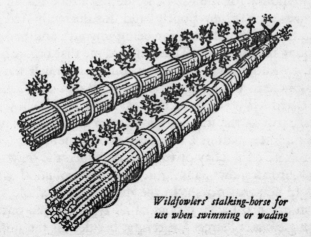

Wildfowlers' stalking-horse for use when swimming or wading

Chapter Nine

IT was three weeks before we returned to Dibin. We travelled north to Baidha, at the upper limit of the Eastern permanent marsh, and then turned eastward again towards Persia, along the dividing line between seasonal and perpetual water. By thus turning at right angles to our course we followed two sides of a great lake unmarked on any map. So wide was it that at the horizon the water met the sky without any dividing line between them, and the black dots of resting waterfowl scattered over the great expanse were difficult to distinguish from slow-moving birds of prey in the air above them. We passed through villages of the Sharanba Tribe, a widely scattered people who number only a few hundred in all, villages that, because of the mosquito-filled reed-beds closely encircling them, would be deserted before the coming of summer. Here the villagers were less friendly and more rapacious; one settlement at the edge of the great lake even tried to charge money for the use of a hunting canoe for an hour, and we were often poorly and insufficiently fed. The reputation of the Ma'dan for being uncouth and boorish is not quite unearned, for Thesiger told me that before he had come to know them he had encountered much the same atmosphere in villages such as Bumugeraifat and Gabab.

We arrived at dusk at one of these villages, by name Sharsh, just as the inhabitants were preparing to leave for their summer quarters a few miles away. There had been no water there until a day or two before, when the thaw of the high Kurdish snows had begun to pour a cool flood over the lands of seasonal marsh. In the morning the whole village was in exodus. Laden canoes of all types moved out from the single water "street", carrying, besides all the goods of the households, reed matting and reed columns for building arches, cut reeds for weaving, chickens, cats, dogs and calves, while the water buffaloes were towed, protesting, behind the canoes of their owners; as we followed the procession the air was full of the particular yodelling cry that urges on the swimming cattle.

Late in the morning we arrived in company with the migrating villagers at the mud island which was their destination. Abu Malih, it was called, "The Father of Salt"; there was so much salt in the soil that the water around it was brackish. There were several hundred yards of flattened earth a yard or so above the level of the water, and every inch of them seethed with human activity. Many of the people had come before us, some of them on the previous day, and there were houses in every stage of construction. All along the banks were drawn up the canoes of the earlier arrivals, and men and women were struggling up the low banks, bent under the load of their cargoes. More canoes arrived every minute, and soon the shallow water at the side from which they had come began to look like a car park outside an English race-track.

As each party arrived and off-loaded their canoes, they would make for the piece of land on which they had staked their claim and at once erect on it, by draping reed matting over an upright canoe pole, a temporary shelter some four feet high. Into this the women carried the cooking pots, and each family had a fire of buffalo dung burning outside the entrance within minutes of arrival. The men and boys laboured to and fro between the canoes and these temporary tents, and before unloading the building materials they would bring up all the household's possessions and stack or scatter them before the entrance to the shelter.

It was possible, in this confusion, to see objects not commonly visible in the dim interior of a stabilised house, and there seemed little variation between the property of one family and another. The most intimate and valuable possessions, such as bangles, clothing, and money, are housed always in a big wooden chest with a domed lid, usually studded with iron or brass, which is normally kept in the women's half of the house. These, as they stood on the bare ground beside the building sites, were the largest solid objects amid a gaudy jumble. There were cushions; blankets of the flaring orange-red that is perhaps the most characteristic of all man-made colours in the marshlands; rugs; an occasional quilt; pots and pans; baskets and trays of close-woven bulrush; fishing spears, and bitumen-headed clubs. Somewhere in each pile lay a corn-grinder, two six-inch-thick discs some two feet across, working on the principle of the upper and the nether millstone, but here the necessary weight was supplied not by stone but by bitumen. A few families owned porous clay water-containers such as are common to houses on the river banks outside the marshes, a long vessel tapering to the lower end and supported by a four-legged wooden stand; and many, too, a clay tray on three legs for burning buffalo dung. Here and there, among the possessions of the few families that owned two or three sheep, were flat ground looms, and wool, raw, spun, and woven, always in the several shades of brown that are the natural colours of the animal. Thesiger told me that he believed there were no local dyes, and that the rugs were made either by the Beni Lam, a pastoral tribe at no great distance, or brought over the frontier from Persia. Most of the weaving in the villages is of the thin hard woollen cloaks that every man wears in the far Eastern Marshes.

The women squatted in the entrances to the shelters and busied themselves with cooking rice for their men or with suckling their babies, and looked out over the stacked household goods to the intense activity all about them. Some of the houses were already complete and looked as if they had stood there for years; some were skeletal frameworks of a gold lighter in tone than the deep blue sky behind them; some were stately rows of straight outward-leaning reed columns, plumed and feathered at their summits, not yet bent together to form arches.

I was able to watch each stage of the building; and to time it, too, for several houses which were not begun when we arrived at 10.30 were complete when we left two hours later. Three or more men worked on each house, and they began by digging, with a spade much like the peat-cutters of the Scottish Highlands, two parallel rows of holes for the feet of the reed arches. Into these holes, two and a half feet deep, they set the base of the long twenty-foot columns in such a way that they leaned outward from the floor-space at an angle of about seventy degrees. Next they made from cut and bound reed bundles a tripod five or six feet high, to be used as we would use a step ladder. Standing on this surprisingly firm and rigid structure a man would reach up and catch with the foot-edge of a spade the upper part of a reed column, bend it down to his own level, and hold it there while he or an assistant reached for the other half of the arch. These two he would bind securely together with twisted lengths of sedge leaf, and move his tripod along to the next column. When the row of five arches was complete, the slenderer bundles of horizontals, fourteen of them in all, connected the whole structure into an integrated anatomy ready for its covering of reed matting. Two hours to build a house—a practical and inexpensive method of prefabrication.

The bustle of building went on for the whole two hours we were there, for new arrivals streamed in incessantly. Through this golden bone-forest of reed columns and house skeletons wandered parties of bellowing buffaloes whose precious dung the children collected as it fell, running with it to the site of their new home. Some of the small boys were naked but for a silver collar set with rock turquoise, the blue stone that has power against the evil eye; they raced and scampered among their preoccupied elders, and splashed and chased each other in the shallow water about the margins of the island.

Though we were able to stay no more than two hours at Abu Malih, I had been fortunate, for not once in his five years among the Ma'dan had Thesiger seen a village in the process of erection.

We could travel only eastward or southward, for there was little marsh water to the north of Abu Malih; one could walk almost dryshod from here to the town of Amara, some thirty miles to the north-west. We kept on due east towards Persia, and we were within a mile or two of the frontier before we turned back on our course. We were now in the territory of the Suwaid, enemies of the Faraijat; we had learned at Abu Malih that there had recently been an exchange of buffalo raids, each raid and robbery followed by a counter-raid into the other's territory.

At Mekri, the next semi-nomad village of buffalo people, the foothills of Khuzistan were crouched and tawny on the horizon. They were far off, for here the marshes extend many miles into Persia, but it was strange to see at last an horizon above the level at which one stood.

I remember Mekri in particular for the great beauty of some of its people, the regularity of their features and the perfection of white and even teeth. In the Suwaid villages there seemed, too, fewer people suffering from eye diseases, possibly fewer in all the Eastern Marshes than in the Central. Among all the Ma'dan the teeth usually appear to be either very bad or very good; they clean them with salt, and the worst mouths may be no more than the effect of negligence, but at Mekri the standard was so near to perfection that the plainest face could be transformed in an instant by a smile. One child I remember in particular; the curve of lips no less perfect than the teeth they covered; the column of the neck from straight slim shoulders, the long shaded eyes that held the gentleness of the gazelle's gaze. There was something moving in the composure of those small shapes wrapped in the hard brown woollen cloaks; in the softness of the faces and the harshness of the work-worn hands; so vulnerable within that armour of beauty.

The very last of these villages, the extremity, as it were, of our eastern journey, was Kirsuwa, a village of no more than seven houses, and it was almost waterless. We had reached it, as we had come to Jeraiwa a week before, through ankle-deep waterways that often petered out into dry land; and a hundred times, it seemed, we had turned back from these blind alleys to make yet another wide detour leading us away from our destination. In the end we had to leave the *tarada* several hundred yards from the houses and walk.

What little water there was here, and it was all that the people had to drink, was literally the colour of pea soup. It lay in small puddles and patches, green, with a dense buff-coloured scum at the edges; in the largest pool, perhaps a hundred yards from the houses, lay a dead buffalo, the hair gone from the stretched hide, through which the white ribs had burst. Two black-and-white crows were excavating the interior with enthusiasm. The flies had become noticeable at the first of the nomad villages; here they were pestilential.

We could go no farther than Kirsuwa, and we turned back westward over the same course, through Mekri and Jidaid and on, still farther west, to the large land village of Baidha. Here there were big trading boats, and the water-ways were alive with many types of craft loading and un-loading. My eye had now grown long accustomed to the wide treeless horizons of the marshes, and accordingly magnified into disproportion any object intruding on the bare skies; here I mistook for a full date grove a verdure that revealed itself on closer approach as half a dozen scrubby dwarf palms in the compound of a *mudhif*. We spent the night there as guests of Ghaghban bin Faleh, son of Faleh bin Fahut, one of the greatest sheikhs of the area. In this *mudhif* there was electric light, and the thumping of the single-stroke engine that produced it took me further back than the few weeks that I had been out of the civilised world; back to childhood and Scotland and the moorland house that had been my early home, where through drowsy summer days that same sound had made a background to a world of sunshine. There were crickets on the floor of the *mudhif*, and during the evening their thin singing was shrill above the chatter of the frogs and the dull thudding of the machine.

I used to find these long evenings in *mudhifs* wearisome, for even when I could understand a little of a conversation I could never join in it, and the easy atmosphere of the common houses was, among the majority of these august people, subdued by formality. It brought me a belated sympathy for a man whom I had known during the war, who had a nervous breakdown because, he said later, I and a brother officer had ignored him. He was a promoted Quartermaster Sergeant, stationed with us as Quartermaster in one of those remote houses on the West Coast of Scotland where agents such as Odette carried out a certain stage of their training before being parachuted into enemy-occupied territory. He was a colourless little man with whom, apart from the accident of educational differences, I doubt if I could have found much in common; and with my other colleague I conversed, I suppose, from a background of tastes and interests that he did not share. So callously unobservant were we that the first symptom we saw was, as far as we were concerned, the last; he appeared one morning at breakfast stark naked and flourishing a service revolver—moreover he was, for some reason that now eludes me, spattered from head to foot with green ink.

I wiled away the time that evening by studying the details of the magnificent *mudhif*, a building that, in striking contrast to the houses at Abu Malih, had taken a hundred and fifty men three weeks to put up. The floor space was sixty-five feet long by twenty wide. There were nine arches, fifteen feet high, and each tied with a hundred and twenty double rings of rope—nearly five hundred yards of rope to every arch, for the average circumference from the yard-thick base of the columns to their tapering tops in the dim ceilings was not less than six feet. Beyond the arches lay the horizontals, a hundred and twenty four-inch-thick reed bundles tied every four inches of their whole length. Another thousand yards of rope. These horizontals continued to within three feet of the floor, below which there was a bare skirt of matting that could be lifted to relieve the heat. A veritable palace of reeds.

As we journeyed north-west the next day we passed through low marsh country where there were patches of green grass and tenuous tentacles of navigable water. The ground and the air were alive with birds of all kinds, and there were small scattered flocks of Sacred Ibis; for some reason it was one of these, rather than hosts of more edible fowl, that the canoe boys demanded should be shot for them. The ibis were, however, wise and wary, and not one came within eighty yards of the *tarada*. The crew chattered at me to shoot at every bird within a quarter of a mile, and eventually, more to put an end to this nuisance than with expectation of ruffling so much as a feather, I fired at a single ibis passing a full hundred yards away on our flank. To my utter astonishment it fell stone dead; it was not until some time later that I realised that the cartridges had got mixed up in my pocket, and that I had accidentally used one containing LG shot, six huge pellets intended for pig shooting.

Kathia leapt from the *tarada* and ran splashing through the ankle-deep water to collect the ibis. When he reached it he drew his curved knife, took his direction from the sun, and, pointing the bird's head to the general quarter where he believed Mecca to be, he began to slit its throat. A cry of dismay came from Hassan—Mecca, he called to Kathia, was much farther to the south. Kathia reorientated himself and began again. This time he was stopped by a yell from Amara, who judged Mecca to be somewhere between the two points so far chosen. Kathia became hopelessly confused, and began to spin like a top, the gashed throat of the dead ibis dripping blood east, west, south and north. Amid cries of derision he returned sulkily to the *tarada*, to be greeted by the flat statement that no one could possibly eat that ibis now. Kathia threw the bird angrily to the bottom of the canoe, and the argument about it was still active in the form of desultory repartee when some half an hour later we passed an old man herding buffaloes on the bank of a waterway. Someone suggested giving the ibis to him, as he would not know that its head had been aimed many degrees off-course when the throat was slit. Kathia tossed it to him with a lordly gesture of largess, but as he did so Hassan began a malicious explanation of why this particular ibis was not lawful food. The old man did not trouble himself with the dispute, merely remarking that in his opinion ibis were quite inedible in any case.

So scrupulous a following of religious custom with so complete an absence of religious observance—for very few of the Ma'dan know more of prayer than is necessary for their buffoonery of it—must be rare in any religion. It is in the matter of food that this aspect is most striking among the marshmen, for they are hedged about with taboos that make no concession to convenience. I never learned, during my short stay among them, the full list of appetising birds, beasts, and fishes that were unlawful meat, but I knew enough to puzzle how these restrictions had begun. The various species of plover that offered a constantly easy target when we were short of food were all unclean; and I had imagined the taboo to extend to all the family of wading birds, until Sabeti chided me one day for not shooting at the bird they call *gus-gus*, the bar-tailed godwit. The fishy tasting pigmy cormorants, no larger than a pigeon, and the great African darter, are both clean; pelicans, which I am told taste little different, are unlawful.

Among fish, catfish are unclean, and all that are shaped like eels, and all shellfish. A pig is of course impossible to any Muslim, but all grazing beasts are lawful. Thesiger told me that beliefs as complex and seemingly without reason are held by the Bedouin of Arabia, among whom it is permissible to eat the Desert Fox but not the Steppe Fox.

The following day I learnt just how difficult it can be to kill a wild boar. We had come to the village of Sijla just before the light began to fade, and took the *tarada* at once to look for pig, accompanied by a young Suwaid in a flat hunting canoe so small as to resemble a water-ski. The country here was all shallow water and bulrushes, with an occasional open lagoon. The rushes were nowhere very thick, and one could see through them to a distance of perhaps a gunshot away. Every now and again we flushed a purple gallinule, the great gaudy blue and purple fowl, as big as the biggest of domestic hens, that takes the place of water-hens in the marshes. The Suwaid found a pig but moved it; we could hear the splosh of its galloping, and we gave chase, the crew paddling with a frenzy of effort. We could not catch up with him while he was in his depth, but should he reach water deep enough to have to swim we should overhaul him easily. We came to a lagoon and he was swimming in front of us; as he reached the shallow water at the far side and his body became visible he was no more than twenty yards from me, and broadside on. I fired one cartridge of LG at his heart and the second at his neck, but he seemed to feel neither. He crossed a belt of foot-deep water among bulrushes, and then he was swimming again and the *tarada* came up on him fast. When we were no more than five yards from him I took the .45 Colt and fired at the back of his neck. I used the whole magazine of thirteen cartridges, and there was no question of a miss, for the impact would have shown in the water. The first seven shots made no impression on him whatsoever; at the eighth he submerged, but after a moment he came to the surface again, still swimming strongly. He showed no signs of feeling the next four of those massive bullets, though I could see each one thud into the matted hair; the thirteenth, and last, chanced to break the spinal column, and then he died instantly. Little hope, I thought, one would have against a charging boar who clung to life like that one.

The half hour's return to Sijla is one of the images that, together with the clamour of the frogs and the black *chevaux de frise* of reeds on sunset skies, I shall carry longest in my memory of the marshes. The sun went down now in a muslin of clouded yellow and dove-grey etched with strings of homing ibis, and against it glided the silhouette of the young Suwaid poling his hunting canoe with a fishing spear. So narrow was his tiny craft that he stood with one foot in front of the other, as much a part of it as a horse's body was part of a centaur. The figure moved with a classic grace, the *dish-dasha* tied around his loins accentuating the slimness of the torso; he leaned backward as the haft end of the spear entered the water, then bent from the waist as he drove down on it with the swift, smooth urgency of the long thrust, a movement as controlled and fluid as that of a ballet dancer. Each time as he straightened again for the next thrust on the other side of the canoe the five points of the spear were black against the sky; the taut silhouette and the slim, dark sliver of the canoe carving in utter silence through the shining liquid sky and sunset-coloured water. Above him a single star began to glitter bright as the moon.

In a few years' time that young tribesman whose urgent silhouette I shall carry in my mind's eye as a symbol of the marshlands will be driving a lorry if he is lucky, pimping in the back streets of Basra for white employees of a western Petroleum Company if he is not.

The frog chatter that night was the loudest that I had heard. The ground was mainly dry round the house, but there were a few pools of water close to the walls, and from these came a babel so loud that it was necessary to raise one's voice to talk in the house. Some of the louder and more cynical frog voices were of such volume that it was difficult to imagine them produced by creatures less than the size of a football. When someone passed by the pools outside there was a sudden quiet in the foreground, in which one could hear the steady roar from the distant reed-beds.

After midnight there was unceasing thunder all through the dark hours, the peals continuing for minutes at a time all round the horizon, and heavy rain streamed through the roof of the house. It began to clear in the morning, and there were windy gleams of sunshine on the scattered water. In the afternoon, when the skies were bare above a rain-washed landscape, we went out again to look for pig, this time in company with five other canoes. Here, between Sijla and Jerait, the country varied from dry desert, where there were traces of recent nomad shepherd encampments, to open water with high reed islands. I travelled in a canoe paddled by two Suwaid, and the fleet soon scattered, so that I knew the directions of the others only by the sound of shooting.

Before that day I had had no conception of the numbers of wild pig that lay concealed in the reed-beds. Like hunting spaniels the five canoes harried them from the thickets until all around us they were galloping over hard ground, swimming in droves through the wide blue lagoons, or standing as dark hulks at the edges of the ochre reed islands. At one moment I could count forty-seven within rifle shot of me. After half an hour I was almost in tears of frustration. Thesiger had lent me his rifle, but I had no means whatever of communicating with the two Suwaid, who, wild with excitement, seemed to think it as easy for me to shoot while the canoe rocked and plunged under the urging of their paddles as if it were motionless on terra firma. Again and again, exactly as I pressed the trigger, the canoe would lurch over to the deep thrust of a paddle and the bullet slam into the water a few yards from us. Then the two Suwaid would steady the canoe for just long enough to give me a deeply reproachful look. When I did at length remember their word for "stop" the results were still more disastrous, for they interpreted the word not as "stop paddling" but as "stop the canoe", and they would begin at once to backwater with a frenzy of strokes that almost tipped me over the side. Standing in the lurching canoe with field-glasses, camera, and revolver all hung round me, clutching the rifle at the ready, I felt like a wobbly Christmas tree, and when the rifle fired it was as if a cracker had gone off unexpectedly. Had it not been for my last three shots of the afternoon my reputation for total inefficiency would have spread quickly through all the surrounding villages. From the direction of Thesiger's canoe, hidden from us by the reed-beds, four half-grown pigs swam in line ahead, crossing our bows a hundred and fifty yards away. As the two Suwaid spotted them and were about to give chase, I saw beside us a little island of mud a few inches above the water. I leapt to it from the canoe, and, starting with the leader, I managed to pick off all four pigs as they swam. To a more sophisticated audience the effect of this display would have been marred by the fact that I fired only three shots, the last killing two pigs simultaneously as their heads came abreast, but to these people, imbued with traditions of economy, this accident was an enormous enhancement. They became wild with excitement, and, leaping ashore to the island, they began to war dance round me, yelling out a chant that, had I been able to understand it, would no doubt have done much to restore my self-respect.

Altogether I had killed eleven pigs with no less than thirty-two cartridges, while Amara had shot the same number with fourteen, and Thesiger had killed one with a shot-gun.

A duck-hunter had arrived home a little before us; he squatted by the coffee hearth with his bag lying before him, the feathers singing in the fire. There were two purple gallinule, two garganey, four pintail, and some coots. Two of the pintail were alive, half in the fire, their heads resting on the headless neck-stumps of the dead.

After that day we were once more among the sheikhs of the outland waterways bordering on desert and cultivating land. The first of these was a young man no less than six feet three inches tall; tall Arabs are so very rare that he seemed a giant. One eye was entirely closed, giving to the face an habitually inscrutable expression. I had by now calculated that, apart, perhaps, from the nomads, one man in every fourteen or fifteen had either lost an eye or suffered from advanced eye-disease.

Here, in the crowd outside the *mudhif*, an old man in a red turban and an ancient khaki coat reaching to his knees carried in his arms a child of about eighteen months. Its face was barely distinguishable as human, the whole skull, down to a point across the cheek-bones, so deeply crusted as to resemble the dried skin of a toad. The eyes were slits in this crust, defined by crimson streaks of the colour that is left by a red Biro pen, continuing across the bridge of the nose in a deep fistula; the cheeks, swollen to the size of a football, were covered with thick scales. The mouth, though quite inhuman, was red as though with rouge. Once I thought I saw a movement within the eye slits; otherwise there was no apparent trace of life. The old man took this terrible creature away after Thesiger had reiterated that he could do nothing for it, and presently he returned alone. The children edged away from him; then, trying to persuade a ten-year-old to dance, the man laid a hand upon his wrist and tried to pull him from his comrades. The child screamed and struggled, and bit the wrist that held him; then suddenly choked and spat.

The next sheikh, Abdullah, was fat and benign, and occupied our horizon for the best part of three days. Unlike most *mudhifs*, his had an atmosphere of cheerful informality, and was dominated, numerically and otherwise, by children. One of these, a fifteen-year-old boy called Daoud, was a superbly accomplished dancer, of a grace, speed, and contortion that the Performing Flea might perhaps emulate in five years' time. He had a far greater repertoire than any other dancer I had seen, and by now we had seen many, yet despite this the only eroticism that appeared in his dances was in those that were anecdotal. He danced for an hour, and when he sat down Abdullah, who had clearly appreciated the performance to the full, muttered something about going to look for a lost buffalo calf. Summoning Daoud to help him, he disappeared into the pitch-black night outside. Twenty minutes later they returned, the sheikh a little breathless and perspiring, but looking pleased and contented. The boy Daoud was smirking; the buffalo calf was not mentioned.

The evening ended with a war dance whose chorus was in praise of Thesiger,

> He does not want a buffalo
> He does not want a hundred sheep
> But his rifle and dagger are deadly.

We moved no more than two hundred yards the next day, to the *mudhif* of Abdullah's brother. Here a holy man in a white turban extended finger-tips in greeting and disdain, and left immediately, presumably to wash his hands; an elderly Sayid took his cue, and I could almost feel him shrink from the touch of the unbeliever. Immediately after a lavish lunch, agonising pains seized Amara's belly; he was in such distress that he could not speak, and he writhed and groaned while Sabeti, to my surprise, began to cry. After a time the pain began to wear off a little, and, doped with opium and belladonna, Amara fell asleep. Sheikh Abdullah, who had come with us to his brother's *mudhif*, seemed to identify himself deeply with Amara, and was soon curled up and snoring heavily opposite to him. He was still asleep when Amara recovered enough for a journey of another few hundred yards to a magnificent *mudhif* of fifteen arches on the opposite bank of the stream, but here Amara collapsed again. Abdullah arrived after us, newly awoken from a *couvarde* not unlike that of North American Indians who go through a simulated confinement when their wives are in labour; he chirruped at Amara, and getting no response he settled down to disconsolate chatter among the rich pillows.

It was a dragging afternoon. I sat next to an English-speaking schoolboy, who asked me, "Are you a very brave man? How far is it from London to Liverpool? How many pigs can you kill?", and, finally, written down for a written reply, "Are you very like us? I ask you." I did not know the answer to any of his questions.

In the evening Daoud danced again. One of his dances was the tale of a man who had seduced another's wife in the reeds and was hauled before the government authorities; they got all the names mixed up and ended by punishing the wrong man. Here, I saw, was the common denominator of the dances that made fun of holy men and of the attitude of prayer; it was a simple mockery of authority.

Another was a dance of fish-spearing; a stranger came on the scene, ate the fish as it was cooking, and was murdered by the spearer. A third man, a policeman, arrived and accused the killer, who brushed the whole matter aside, saying, "He must have been dead for days; and anyway why bother about trivial rubbish of that sort?"

After all the dancing was over Sheikh Abdullah looked frustrated, as though he wished he had lost another buffalo calf, or perhaps several. He consoled himself by talking of a neighbour who, he said, had four wives and forty-six concubines, and satisfied six of them every night.

Marshmen's daggers

Chapter Ten

I WOKE the next morning giddy and with a slight fever. It was the only sickness that I suffered throughout all the journey; for three days I felt unsteady and stupid in the daytime, and at night my dreams were of things unhappy and far off. Thesiger, too, was unwell, and lost his voice; our symptoms were perhaps related to Amara's collapse the day before. We had moved a mile or two to another stone fort, and here I was saddled for nearly three hours with the headmaster of the local school. It would have been a difficult enough time had I had my wits about me; in the dull state to which the fever had flattened me it was little less than torture. Thesiger introduced him to me as a gesture of kindness, thinking that it would be a relief for me to be able to speak English to somebody. After the first few minutes of deadlock, he sent a boy to fetch from his house *The Oxford University Top Book*. This proved to be an English Primer, complete with pictures of cats, mats, and other monosyllabic riff-raff dear to the nursery. For a solid hour he read aloud from this volume, infinitely slowly, and "putting in the expression".

"Is the cat on the table?" he read slowly and probingly. "No!"—archly—"the cat is *under* the table!" "Is the boy work-ing? *No!* He is play-ing with his elder sister's dug!" At this point I interjected: "Doing *what?*" and he passed me the book with an aggrieved air; there was a picture of a child in shorts playing with an Aberdeen terrier. The primer had not been prepared for use in a Muslim country. At last he closed the book and said sententiously, "Of all the c's that werbi this c that. Yes?" Seeing me look blank he repeated it, and then wrote it down. I took his English-Arabic dictionary and found the word for "quotation". "Is it a quotation?" I asked. He nodded enthusiastically. "I think," I said painfully, "that there must be something missing."

He turned to me with a sudden brightness. "My father is underground," he remarked with an air of surprise, by way of changing the conversation. It was clear that we should always be at cross purposes.

Two days later we drove by car to the town of Amara. Thesiger had sent a messenger to order a taxi, and it appeared magically on the opposite bank of the stream to the *mudhif* at which we were staying. There was no sign of a road anywhere; for a mile or so we bumped and zigzagged across dry uncultivated land traversed by waterless irrigation ditches, and when the road began it was at first a barely perceptible track on the hard mud. Gradually the track grew higher and became a straight mud road running parallel to the bank of the watercourse from which we had set out. On our right, as we drove north, a vast marsh with lagoons of open water stretched away for many miles; then this gave place to green patches of half-grown barley and wheat, and limitless acres of mud desert dotted with isolated palm groves. We passed many of the Beni Lam nomads, either encamped in black tents with their great sheep flocks spread over seemingly pastureless ground, or on the move with almost as many little laden donkeys as there were sheep.

The town of Amara, at the end of the ten-mile drive, did not live up to the beauty of its name. Yellowish brick and corrugated iron; perpetual peeling enamel advertisements for popular western products; dirt and refuse; everything, after the wide clean skies and astringent life of the marshes, seemed to me shoddy, mean and ugly. We paid courtesy visits to the *muttaserrif*, or provincial governor, and to the Chief of Police, and we visited the American Mission where I was impressed by Dr. Nyekirk, a craggy, rock-jawed young American with a handshake like a gorilla; it was to him that

Thesiger sent from the marshlands patients whom he was unable to treat himself. We lunched, at a building something between a fort, house, and palace, with one of Mehsin's grandsons, the son of that Dakhil whom Aboud had killed in a shooting accident. Our host was doing his national service as a private soldier; according to custom, however, a payment of £50 had reduced the obligatory period to three months.

Very few of the marsh tribesmen do national service at all. They have their own ingenious way of dodging conscription; they will pay a neighbour to borrow a child who is obviously below the requisite age, and this child impersonates the boy who is to be called up. This, though absolutely safe for the recruiting official's first visit, breeds some confusion when he returns, say two years later. Another child is borrowed; sometimes he is even younger than the previous one. The official expresses wonder and amazement at the ingenuous Peter Pan, and a dispute begins. It ends as such arguments are best settled; a little money changes hand, and the incident is closed.

We returned from Amara to another village, to which Hassan and Kathia had transported the *tarada* in our absence, and from there we began to work back, by a different route, to Dibin. The weather was like April in England, with a fresh gusty breeze and the sun shining whitely between glinting showers. The waterways led at first through pastoral country, where encamped nomads tended great herds of cattle and sheep. This was the one moment of the year when the land has a strangely vivid freshness, a tenderness of green that transforms the flat grey wastes into brilliant acres of young grass growing in watery soil. Upon it grazed sheep of all colours, but colours of a peculiar richness, piebald, skewbald, black, brown, and white, and with them were great numbers of Jersey-coloured cattle; as it began to rain the attendant cow-herds, instead of adding more clothing, took off their *dish-dashas* and were naked, with their garments folded into bundles on their heads. A cantering colt splashed at the water's edge, bucking and throwing up his heels in the same exuberance of spirit as the herd-boys who danced in the light gleaming rain; above them the air was rustling with the passage of migrating birds, straggling mile-long flights of little red hawks, green-and-bronze bee-eaters, and the winking black and white of avocets and stilts. Away to the south of us a great flock of wild geese were spiralling down to alight, the golden bugles of their voices drifting thin and clear across the intervening miles of marsh. As we went farther the waterways became choked by a floating carpet of white and gold water buttercups, so thick that in places whole lagoons were completely covered, without an inch of visible water. "There are two pronounced seasons," Thesiger had written in the article that had led me here, "summer and winter, for spring and autumn last only about a month." This was the spring, and it was more glorious than I had seen in any other land.

Here we were in the country of the Sudan; once a great tribe, but now dwindling and scattered, for the building of the Kut barrage had affected the fortunes of all these people dependent upon the distributaries of the great river. We stopped for the night at the fort of Sheikh Hatim ibn Saihut, in a palm grove where salmon-pink hoopoes flitted among the branches. It was a building of a type new to me, a vast low structure of mud and brick with walls four feet thick. The reception room was pillared at the centre with three smooth palm trunks, each carrying a square pediment at the summit, where they supported a ceiling of palm beams with reed matting showing between them. In place of the abominable European arm-chairs of most sheikhs' reception rooms there were long seats of dark wood with arms at their ends, and on the floor were scattered a profusion of rich rugs and carpets.

Here we heard news of the controversy between Nasr and

Salman. It was rumoured that Nasr would lose his case in Baghdad, and that the Government would restore his property to his father. Sheikh Hatim told us that Nasr had appealed to him and to many other sheikhs for help, but they had all given him the same reply. They had told him that if he would throw himself on his father's mercy they would go with him and intercede for him, for that was the only course that could retrieve anything of his lost honour. Hatim said again and again that it was outside anyone's experience that a son should defy his father to the unthinkable point of seeking Government aid against him.

After we lay down to sleep the room in the fort was noisy with the courting of swallows, whose mud nests plastered the palm beams and pillars; all through the night they sang and made love, the clear silver bubbling of their voices loud in the darkness. The beam of an electric torch would silence them for a moment; they would draw guiltily apart like lovers in Hyde Park caught in the beam of a car's headlights, but as soon as the light left them they were at it again, vocal and irrepressible.

If I had accepted Thesiger's statement that an unwounded wild boar would charge a man unprovoked I had accepted it as a child believes the existence of death; it was not a thing that could have any personal significance for me. I had seen the terrible wounds inflicted by pig, a long scar puckering a brown thigh from knee to groin, a back cross-furrowed by hideous laceration, the calf of a leg that must once have hung in tatters from the bone. I knew indeed that nearly half of all the Ma'dan men carried such scars in some degree.

The stories, however, were all either of wounded pig or of a sleeping beast surprised suddenly by a reed cutter or a fish spearer as he waded, often waist deep, through the reeds; or of a small canoe coming unaware upon one of the little soggy reed islands which the pig build to sleep on. The picture was always one of a startled animal surprised from sleep by an enemy already on top of him, or of a wounded animal in whom the dull embers of pain smouldered into explosive flame at the approach of its inflictor. To reinforce my euphoric security there was the fact that I had by now killed quite a few pig myself; none had charged me nor displayed anything but fear, and further the marshmen had shown little caution in following into thick reed-beds pigs that we did not know to be dead. On only one point was I not deluded, the ubiquity of pigs. They were as common as rabbits in England before myxomatosis was introduced, and in my secret view I thought, perhaps, that they were little more dangerous. I needed a lesson, and I got one.

We left the fort of Sheikh Hatim that morning to return to Malaya. There were heavy blue-grey clouds all round the horizon, with a mutter of distant thunder and the threat of rain, and my temper matched the sky. It is not easy for two men to travel alone, as did Thesiger and I, unless they know each other very well, and that morning my mind was filled with fancied grievances against him, with the marshalling of trivialities into an orderly assault force. Thesiger was among friends and I was among strangers, and I felt isolated and frustrated. The mood was perhaps not dignifiable by any other name than sulks, but it had not lifted when later in the morning the skies cleared and the sun came out and lit the pale sheets of water and the vivid greens of new growth. We left the dry land behind us and the nomads with their black tents and great sheep herds, and at length there was once more water on both sides of the low canal. It had not been there long, for the reed growth was short and scattered, no more than a foot or two high and thin like lace, so that the extending water showed always through it and beyond it to where the hills of Khuzistan hunched low and curiously pale on the horizon. A group of two or three smuggling boats passed us, the towers on the bank bent and straining as they hauled the heavy boat-loads of contraband grain from over the Persian frontier. There was an ostentatious display of firearms throughout the party. It crossed my mind vaguely that this was the first day for a long time that our rifles were not carried loaded and ready to hand, but I was feeling too flat and sullen to comment upon it.

Not far off to our left an enormous concourse of duck were on the wing and wheeling. They wanted to return to the point from which they had risen, a few hundred yards away, and as I watched they began to pour in again, moving the water with a liquid roar as they alighted in drove after drove. The air above them was a wild weaving throng of wings as the racing packs checked to alight, hurtled downwards, then shot up again. A party would alight, rest tense and motionless with upstretched necks, then take off again in panic, but their places on the water were instantly filled by others. Round the restless throng of pintail, shoveller and wigeon long clouds of teal described dazzling arcs of speed a few feet above the water; one moment they were dark as driven smoke, the next as they wheeled in unison their undersides showed silver as a shoal of darting herring.

Thesiger saw me watching them. "There won't be much to eat where we're going," he said. "Do you think you could do anything with those? Probably bread and some milk otherwise."

I looked at the place where the duck were alighting. They seemed to want to stay there, but there didn't seem enough cover to hide a mouse, let alone a man. Still, I would be out of the canoe, I would be able to straighten my aching knees, and I would be quite alone for the first time for many weeks. It would feel like freedom. I could think without being overheard. I said, "I might. I'll try. But once I put them up they won't come back while the *tarada*'s anywhere around. You'd have to take her at least half a mile farther on, give me half an hour and then come back."

"All right—here's six cartridges. What are you going to do for cover?"

"I'll find something," I said enigmatically. I had been a wildfowler in my youth, and I fancied myself to get duck where the next man could not. As I stepped from the canoe to the mud bank of the canal Thesiger said, "Don't waste all those cartridges firing wild shots."

As the canoe pushed off into the channel again I sat down on the mud bank and began to roll up my trousers. It was hopeless, I knew; one could roll them tight and high as a pair of bathing drawers, but in five minutes they would come cascading down again, and the next time one rolled them one would be finding mixed clay and water clammy against the inside of the thigh. With a *dish-dasha* one had only to hitch it up and tie it round the waist. I finished and stood up; the trousers might be good for a hundred yards. The duck were mostly gone now; only an odd bird circled far out of range, and a pelican sailed by on stiff wings, stately as a battleship.

My plan was to get to the area where the duck had been, and squat down there, if necessary up to the waist in water, to wait for their probable return. There was, I saw, a very little cover which might be made to serve—not far from where I wanted to be there was a lump of earth about eighteen inches high, possibly the corner of a submerged earth dyke, and some way beyond it there was another, even smaller. The nearer was about two hundred and fifty yards from where I stood.

I left the canal bank and began to wade to it. The water came to a little below my knees, and the clay bottom was soft and gripping, with a prickle of burnt reed stubble that hurt the bare soles of my feet. My mind went off on the tack that was its childish favourite that morning. "Thesiger has canvas commando boots for this, but he never told me to bring a pair." Buffalo had been on this ground before it was flooded, their deep footprints made treacherous potholes, and the bump of the camera on my chest reminded me that if I slipped once I might not be able to take any more photographs at all.

Halfway, and the cuffs of my trousers flopped down into

the water; I took a masochistic pleasure in the cold grip of the wet clay at my groin as I rolled them up again. I noticed that the sole of my right foot was bleeding quite a lot. A few duck had returned and were circling; I loaded my gun and went on. When they had gone the sky was great and empty and blue with one long plume of white cloud lying right across it.

I was about fifty yards from the lump of mud when I came to what looked like a ditch. Elsewhere the low green reeds were scattered, thin and irregular, but here was a defined belt perhaps a couple of paces across in which no reeds grew. I tested it cautiously with one foot, thinking it might be deep, but it wasn't. The water reached just above my knee; I took a pace forward with the other foot.

At that moment I looked up. I had not, I think, heard anything; I was merely re-orientating myself upon my course. A little beyond and to the right of the lump of mud, and about eighty yards from me, was a very large wild boar. That was all my mind registered at first—surprise that so large an animal should have appeared where there had been no cover to hide it before. Next I noticed that the boar was facing me head-on and that it was moving. These stages of realisation must each have lasted a very, very short time, but they were quite clearly defined stages before the full impact of realisation came at me, and with it my heart came up into my mouth: the boar was charging me, and we were all alone, he and I, two little dark specks out in the glittering waste of water, the one stationary and afraid and the other. . . .

The gun. It came to me quite suddenly that I had a gun, that I was perfectly safe, that I could kill this creature that was coming to kill me. I almost laughed with relief. Then, even as I brought the gun forward to a ready position, I remembered that the cartridges I was carrying were not LG for pig but No. 5 shot for duck. The gun was useless, or almost useless. Mentally, I panicked, but my feet stood still. Infinitely far away behind me I heard a confused sound of voices shouting. The boar seemed still a long way off, but getting nearer quickly.

I remembered all that Thesiger had told me; I was surprised that I could think so clearly when I was so very much afraid. "If you ever get caught with a charging pig and duckshot in the gun, for God's sake don't do what the Arabs do and waste your ammunition in a panic when the pig's twenty yards away. It'll only sting him up and make him madder. You can't stop him anyway, and you're going to get badly hurt anyway, but you may not get killed if you keep your head. Wait till he's not quite touching you and shoot between his eyes and fall on your belly so he can't get his tusks in your guts. Never fall on your back."

That reminded me that the camera would be wrecked; even at this stage my appreciation of the situation was evidently incomplete. I think the pig was still forty or fifty yards away by the time all this had gone through my head and been arranged into a knowledge of what I had to do: to stand still and let that great hulk gather pace and momentum until its tusks were almost touching me, then to shoot between its eyes and throw myself sideways on my belly into the water. The whole procedure seemed futile, and already my flesh was shrinking and cowering from the cut of the tusks. When I had killed my first boar I had been astonished by the structure of those tusks, totally unprepared for the long knife edge at their sides.

I could see them by now, though for some reason I only remember one, the boar's left tusk. He seemed all shoulders and head, massive like a bull, his hindquarters obscured. He was throwing up a white splash of water all round him, and he was getting very near. Then I saw his tail go up over his back in the final concentrated sprint that was going to kill me. I started to bring the gun up and to shift into a more comfortable stance, but I found that my feet had bogged down into the clay and I had to wrench them free. I was feeling sick with fright as I took two paces back into the shallower water behind what, such ages ago, I had at first taken to be a ditch.

I brought the gun up to my shoulder and sighted between the boar's eyes. He was about fifteen paces away, and I know now that when a charging boar is only fifteen paces away he seems to be already on top of you. It took every vestige of self-control I had not to fire then. Ten yards. Five. After all I wasn't going to let him touch me before I fired—I was going to shoot when he reached the opposite side of the "ditch", the little reedless strip of water out of which I had stepped backward. That would be something between two and three yards from the muzzle of my gun. And then he was there and I was shooting, but even as I shot I realised that the gun was no longer aiming between his eyes.

At first I didn't realise what had happened; I had been so keyed up for that moment that I had been unable to take in the last-minute change in the situation or to understand the freak of chance that had saved me. I had fired without realising that I was already out of danger, or that to fire could, logically, only lead me back into it. At the peak of his final sprint, when he was no more than three yards from me, the boar had reached the little strip of reedless water that separated us. A pig is never aggressive when out of his depth, and, like me before him, he must have taken this strip for a deep ditch. He swerved left along its bank with the full speed of his charge, and the shots that I had been too strung up to prevent myself from firing had taken him just behind the shoulder, right over the heart. A dark patch like a hole sprang out on his hide, but he gave no sign of feeling it; he galloped on across the shallow water, heading to cross the canal a hundred yards or so beyond the distant *tarada*.

It was over. In all, it had lasted less than half a minute. I was left in a tremendous vacuum of anti-climax.

Over at the canoe there was a lot of confused activity. Thesiger's shouting voice came to me on the breeze; the rifles were buried among the baggage and were not loaded;

the pig had crossed the canal and was galloping across semi-dry country on the other bank before he could take his first hurried shot. A miss, and so was the second, but the third, when the boar was some three hundred yards away and going at full speed, hit him somewhere behind the ribs. After that he was almost tail-on and small in the distance, and there was nothing more to be done.

I found myself unable to feel my usual sympathy for a wounded animal, indeed I felt nothing about it at all except regret that I was unable to see how far my point-blank shot had penetrated, and that I could not keep as memento those tusks that had so very nearly been in me. (In fact this would have been impossible anyway, as their extraction would have involved an insuperable amount of "uncleanness".) My attitude towards wild pig had changed.

So had my attitude to lumps of mud that provided convenient cover for duck-flighting. There was only one now, where before I had seemed to remember two. I examined it very carefully and suspiciously before I resumed my interrupted wade. It was, however, a genuine lump of mud, very wet and sticky, and it would not give cover or camouflage until I had immersed myself in the water almost to the waist and embraced its clammy hulk with the rest of my body. Presently a garganey came streaking over my head and I missed it; it was not a satisfactory position from which to shoot. I considered the situation; up to the present, I thought, my dignity had been little impaired in the eyes of the onlookers, for they had had no means of knowing how extremely frightened I had been, but to squat here tied in cold clippery knots and miss a lot of duck would strike a false note. The *tarada* showed no signs of leaving, and after a while I uncoiled myself and hailed Thesiger across the water.

"Do you think it's worth waiting?"

There was no reply, so I said it again, several times. The reply when it did come was indistinct and baffling. It sounded like "You bloody fool!"

I picked and sloshed my way wearily back to the *tarada*. Thesiger was in the best of good humours, and the canoe boys were chattering like monkeys; each of them insisted on kissing me ardently. Sabeti's moustache tickled.

"What a' man!" said Thesiger. "Here he is, charged by a boar from an unprecedented distance, absolutely no right to be alive at all, saved by some extraordinary miracle that deflects the boar at the last possible second—and then, when he's safe, he has to go and *fire* at it with No. 5 shot! You really *are* a bloody fool! It was nothing but another miracle that he didn't turn straight back at you. Well, well! Do you know I became quite fond of you when I saw you were going to be killed? I realised that I should definitely miss you when you'd gone. And then he walks on and wallows about in the mud like a hippo and misses a perfectly easy duck. Extraordinary fellow—quite mad. Anyway, I was very glad you didn't panic and run away; we should never have been able to hold up our heads in the marshes again if you had. . . . Do you know I couldn't help wishing in a way that he'd got you?—nothing personal, I mean, but I've never seen that happen before, and I wanted to see what he'd do to you. Incomplete, somehow. . . . Still, isn't it true what I said about one's not being frightened when one's charged? There just isn't time to be, is there?—I knew you'd find it so."

I tried, in the interests of an analytic honesty, to explain that I had rarely if ever been more afraid in my life, but that the idea of turning my back on those murderous tusks and letting them out of my sight had been an even more unthinkable horror. Thesiger, I think, did not understand; I doubt whether he has ever experienced physical fear, as I know it, in his life. "No, no," he said, "one can tell—you didn't run away."

Just as well, I thought; he would have had no respect for me had he known all that had gone on in my head during those long seconds.

Chapter Eleven

MY encounter with the boar exercised a profound effect upon my outlook. Perhaps it was because I no longer felt myself to be so perfect a cypher; at last one living creature in all this alien waste of water and sky had really taken notice of me, had thought me important enough to be worthy of destruction. It gave me some ecological status, as it were, even to be the target of a charging pig.

From the beginning my idleness had irked me; I had been a passenger par excellence. Perhaps for the first time in my adult life I had been responsible for nothing, neither for the least decision nor for the carrying out of the simplest piece of the party's routine. Leisure has little appeal when all free-will action is removed from it, and indeed to light a cigarette was about all the free-will action I could perform without co-operation. Ordinary physical movement was almost completely inhibited, for I had had perforce to spend the greater part of my time either cross-legged in the bottom of a war canoe or cross-legged on the floor of a house. Even when we were not afloat, to take a walk, literally to stretch one's legs, was out of the question, either because there was no land to walk on, or, when there was a dry-land village with hard earth between the houses, because of the savage dogs that patrolled the perimeter of every dwelling. Because of them one could not even leave a house to relieve oneself without announcing one's intention and taking an armed guard who stood over one grotesquely the while.

This extreme restriction upon physical activity and lack of preoccupation with any responsibility did, I think, make me more mentally alert and observant than normally, but on the other hand its total effect was a feeling of reduction to the status of a child, with concomitant resentment and frustration. Like a child, too, I often understood little of what the adults were talking about, and in the long evenings I had found that much of the charm of studying a circle of forty firelit faces is lost when one realises that each of the forty faces is studying one's own. Now my narrow escape had at the same time satisfied a need of my own and made me the object of a more flattering interest.

We stopped that night at Abumilih, a small densely built village of the Sudan tribe, on both high banks of a narrow, road-wide watercourse. We were still some ten miles north of the edge of the permanent marsh, and cultivating country stretched out beyond the confines of the villages, most of it still bare and arid-looking, for the water had not yet come. The village was noisy, noisier than any of the marsh villages, where the houses are less closely clustered; to the usual thunder of the dogs and the hoarse cries of their owners was added the cackling and trumpeting of a great number of domestic geese. One of the first things I noticed after we had scrambled up the steep canal bank into the waiting swarm of villagers was a brood of young chickens two or three days old. They were round as puffballs, and every one, from head to toe, was a brilliant aniline green. They looked very fabulous, and their dun-coloured hen fussed over them as though conscious of the rarity and importance of her charges. At first I thought this pleasing folly the work of a child, and was reminded momentarily of a revolting purple Pekinese that I had once seen languish into Claridge's at the heels of a startling Parisienne. As I looked up from these ridiculous pieces of Disney animation, however, I found myself staring into the soft moon faces of a row of young calves. They were tied halter to halter, so that the slack loops of rope draped evenly and stylistically between their heads, and at the forehead of each, where there should have been a splash of white, flared a vivid patch of magenta. Beyond them stood a heifer with a magenta udder and green teats. It was the time of the New Year by the Persian calendar, and these were potent charms against the Evil Eye.

This Evil Eye is not, as far as I could understand, a personal thing, lying in the power of an evil individual, but in a general sense the eye of evil and harm, the regard of malign powers. The brightly coloured animals appear an anomaly, however, for among the people themselves one infers that it must be the uninteresting, the insignificant or ugly, that escapes the attention of evil powers. Thus a child who is the successor to several who have died is often called by the name of something unpleasant or trivial, so that attention may be diverted from him, and the family escape further victimisation. Extreme names of this type are those of the most unclean objects that exist; parents in a panic through infant mortality may condemn their child to carry for ever the name "Pig", or "Dog", "Jackal", or even "Shit". Less extreme, and with the desire for anonymity among a host of similar insignificant objects, are such names as "Plate", "Date" and "Coffee-cup". I was surprised at the audacity of naming a boy Habib, which means Beloved, until I learnt that he was the youngest of five living brothers.

I learn that the Chinese use somewhat the same means of diverting malign attention from their children, giving to the boys female names and dressing them in girls' clothes to deceive the evil spirits.

Personal charms, what the Italians call *"porta fortuna"* and English Catholics call medals, are of great importance to all the tribesmen, as seems general among many superstitious peoples, but they are used most particularly in childhood and in sickness. Sometimes a family may have quite a collection of these objects tucked away in the wooden chest that holds all their intimate belongings; occasionally there are enough for every member of the family to wear one in the case of a local epidemic. They vary a good deal in type. Wandering Sayids, parasitic as only holy men can be, play upon their supposed status as descendants of the Prophet to sell to the villagers charms against illness, which, if the Sayid concerned is literate, may be a crudely written verse from the Qu'ran, or, if he is illiterate, a few meaningless squiggles that the tribesmen will hold in pathetic respect and awe. Occasionally one sees relics of what may be an earlier magic. At Bumugeraifat, in the Central Marshes, a boy with a low fever carried as a pendant round his neck a pierced round stone the size of a dove's egg, dark, heavy, and very highly polished. Now there is no stone in the marshes, nor for a long way outside them, and by the appearance of this object it was of considerable antiquity in its present form. Thesiger was not with me that day, and my Arabic vocabulary was very small, but I managed to ask where it had come from and to understand that it had been dug up below one of the houses of the village. It seemed to me that it might be very old indeed, and that it might, too, throw some light on the remote and uncertain origins of the people, for the stone was unusual and its nearest *locale* should not be difficult to establish. I tried to buy it from the boy's mother, and when she refused I thought she was bargaining. At length she turned down an offer that left me in no doubt that she was not, the *fus* simply was not for sale; and that, among so poor a people, where practically every material object has its surprisingly low price, was striking evidence of its significance in their eyes. I had seen another, of a bluer, more slaty stone, tied with some other charms into the greasy ends of a woman's headcloth, the domineering yet whiny matriarch of the *mudhif* at Dibin where Sheikh Jabir had war-danced while the eagle owl blinked in the friendly gloom within. She had offered, characteristically, to exchange it for the gold-and-enamel Persian charm that I wore myself, but here my scientific curiosity had become confused by superstitions and sentiments of my own.

It was not until I finally returned to Basra that I acquired one of these stones. I was crossing the wooden bridge to the *suq* when I noticed an old beggar squatting at the corner of the bridge and the canal bank. He was very ragged; he wore the rough woollen *bisht* of a tribesman, and apparently no *dish-dasha* below it, for where it was torn his naked skin showed through it. The *bisht* was open at the chest, and on a mat of white hair lay an oval stone stranger than any I had seen before. I made my way back over the bridge to the workshop of a Sabian with whom I had recently dealt, and explained to him what I wanted. He came across the street with me and from a discreet distance I indicated the stone. He shook his head. "He not sell," he said, and added an Arabic sentence that was too complicated for me. He saw that I did not understand, and tried again, in English. "From before . . . from very very before . . . *kulish, kulish,* strong holy, no sell. Finish." "Try," I said, "and also ask from where it comes. I will wait for you in the shop." He came back after a few minutes, rubbing the stone on the palm of his hand. "Four dinar," he said, "I take one—five, yes? He Ma'dan from other side Qurna. *Fus*—from his father."

I wondered how much the beggar had received for his father's charm, and hoped that it was at least half of the price the Sabian had mentioned. It was not difficult to understand how this stone had acquired a magic status, for it was an unusual and striking object in itself. It seemed like some kind of agate, opaque blue-grey with dark lines in it, and over all one side the distribution of colour formed an almost perfect eye; a blind eye, for the pupil was not defined, and there was a just perceptible milky film over it, as though it was the eye of a dead animal grown cold, the eye of a young calf or a gazelle. As I looked at it there came to me the words of a poem from a different landscape.

> "I was the dying animal
> Whose cold eye closes on a jagged thorn,
> Whose carcass soon is choked with moss,
> Whose skull is hidden by the fern."

How great a part witchcraft and magic play in the life of the people I was unable to discover, nor was Thesiger able to help me. If it is prevalent it would belong to the women's side of life, and that would be virtually impossible for any man, more especially a white man, to explore thoroughly. The very superstitious nature of the people would incline one to believe that it must play a large part. With this outlook events usually tend to form a circle; minor and major ills are attributed to spells, and this in turn encourages emulation by those who would wish to cast them.

Of our four canoe boys only Sabeti admitted wholeheartedly to belief in all *djinns*, but at least two of the others were quite plainly giving the response which they considered our own sophistication to demand; and the fourth, who was more prepared to find a natural explanation for unknown phenomena, was found to believe with childlike simplicity in circumcision by angels. This is an extraordinarily wide-spread belief among tribesmen, and is held even by minor sheikhs who have had at least some contact with western science. Our host proudly told us that he himself had been thus circumcised, and swore by Hussein that he had with his own eyes seen boys of three or four years lying still asleep in the morning with the severed foreskin on the pillow beside their heads and blood at the site of the cut. The most obvious explanation for this belief, that of convenience in the avoidance of an unpleasant operation, is not valid, for it is not a lawful circumcision by their custom, and those thus singled out for miraculous surgery must usually have a little more removed by human agency to make their condition acceptable to the community. Even our host admitted that the angels were not conspicuously efficient at this work, though in fact he himself had undergone no further operation. He became irritated at our obvious scepticism about angels with scalpels.

"There are boys here in this very *mudhif* with us who have been so visited by the angels! Here, Daoud, show them what the angels did!" A boy of about twelve stepped over to us and without embarrassment lifted his *dish-dasha*. The appearance was at first sight misleading, but was in fact quite obviously within the limits of individual variation.

"See!" cried our host, "if we believe in Allah, whom we cannot see, why should we not believe in this which we can see with our eyes? And where was it lying?"

"On the pillow," said the boy dutifully. I thought his voice lacked conviction.

"There! So it was also with me. And in your country is there then nothing that you cannot understand?"

Thesiger began a lengthy statement which I could not follow. Presently he stopped and turned to me. "I was telling them about flying saucers," he said somewhat apologetically.

The company appeared keenly interested; all of them, it appeared, had seen flying saucers. These were quite small, white, and moved very slowly and soundlessly across the sky. Sometimes they would be in sight for twenty minutes or more. They were rather sausage-shaped than saucer-shaped, it emerged from Thesiger's questioning, and they were by no means rare; perhaps we should see one in the morning. Clearly they were no stranger than many other unexplained phenomena.

In fact we did see one in the morning. Excited cries brought us to the door of the *mudhif* before we had finished breakfast. Hands were pointing, eyes were shaded. There wasn't a cloud in the whole sky, and it was still pale blue before the heat of the day. Two sea-eagles were twisting and diving upon each other in play far above us; otherwise I could see nothing. Then I saw what the people were pointing at. It was a minute silver vapour-trail from an aircraft flying at stratospheric height. As they had said, it was quite noiseless.

"It is an aircraft," I said. There were cries of denial and

derision. I went back into the *mudhif* and fetched my field-glasses. Even with a magnification of sixteen the aircraft was only just visible, and was so far away that it seemed to be practically stationary, but it formed a speck of the right shape. I handed the glasses to our host. After a moment he returned them with a slightly disgruntled air. I was not absolutely certain what he said, but I thought it was, "I did not require these things to see what was on the pillow."

Whether or not they admit it, the great majority of the marshmen are afraid of *djinns*, and afraid of the darkness that may hide them. A *djinn* is not, as readers of the better known Arab fiction might suppose, something that always appears out of a bottle, a malign or beneficent creature of enormous power; it is, in fact, any manifestation of the supernatural, for anything not readily explicable is assumed to be the work of some *djinn*. The invisible world is peopled with a great multitude of these beings, and though Mahommed is held to have converted the evilly disposed *djinns*, the great majority of them are still frightening and destructive. They are credited with much greater powers than are "ghosts" in European countries, and are quite often capable of inflicting death. There is one such who is quite generally recognised in the marshes, and held in especial dread. He appears, I think, only at night, and the first that the traveller sees of him is a light, quite small, and by no means unusual or alarming. As the victim draws nearer the light begins to glow more intensely until at last it is huge and blinding and from the centre of it there appears the *djinn*, a giant negro slave, quite naked, and some fifteen or twenty feet high. Some who have seen the *djinn* may live to speak of it after-wards, but they are blighted mentally and physically, their limbs withered and their brains deranged. One of our canoe boys said he had seen this light from a distance more than once, but, knowing it for what it was, had gone no nearer. There may perhaps be gases in the marshes that produce a will o' the wisp or Jack o' Lantern, but the general acceptance of the giant negro slave must owe its origin to one man's raving; not, one feels, to a racial guilt conscience.

A few of the rare tumulus islands in the marshes are said to be haunted, and at least one to hold buried treasure guarded by a fearful *djinn*; but it would seem that it is the darkness of which the marshmen are really frightened, and the whole obscurity of the night rather than any particular places that they tend to people with mischievous spirits.

We left Abumilih early next morning, through narrow, blind watercourses with high mud banks. On either side the land beyond the bank stretched away desolate and bare, the dead grey mud of cultivating land where as yet no green showed nor any water lay, but in front of us palm trees showed a mile or so ahead, and soon we turned into a wider channel whose beauty was breathtaking. Again and again I noticed it in the marshes and in the cultivating land around them—how enormously the impact of colour and verdure is heightened by the contrast that has gone before it, so that a single orange homespun blanket spread to dry on the side of a reed house may take on the splendour of an imperial robe, a single green tree hold the glory of a thousand returning springs, the mystery of eternal forests. To no part of the earth can spring bring transfiguration as it does to the flat lands of the Tigris and Euphrates. In the juvenescence of the year came Christ the tiger.

The waterway into which we turned now seemed Eden itself. On either bank grew groves of date palms, and in the spaces between them a riot of blossom spread against a sky of unbroken turquoise. Feathery golden acacia made a lattice-work against that blue, the vivid flowers flaring in the slant of a sun that was not yet high, and low over the water that reflected the sky with the sheen of enamel trailed weeping trees, some with a crimson flower and some with a white. It was the simple primary colours stippled upon the background of green growth that made the perfection; yet in the transient flash of wings were added wilder and more gorgeous hues. Across the water flickered the halcyon kingfishers, electric blue and chestnut and red, and from palm to palm in undulating flight flew rollers of unbelievable splendour, a flutter of pale blue and purple. Overhead, in the empty patch of sky above the water, a single flamingo flew southward, the sun catching the sheet of blood-colour under his wings.

Even the canoe boys seemed not quite unmoved; Sabeti leaned forward and touched me on the shoulder between strokes of the paddle.

"Zayn hinna, Gavin?"

"Na'am, kulish zayn." It was simple to have a limited vocabulary; I did not have to try to put my confused thoughts into words.

To Thesiger I said idly: "I should like to build a reed house on that bank and live here."

"The Iraqi government wouldn't allow you to."

No, one could not be allowed to build and live in Eden. One could look and perhaps remember, and in time the memory would lose its brilliance. Others were living in Eden, for there were scattered houses throughout the palm grove, but some were empty and abandoned. Their owners, perhaps, had seen Eden in the nearest oil-well or in the scrubby streets of Amara; for here, far north and outside the permanent marshlands, we were in the periphery of western influence.

The palm groves lasted for perhaps a mile, and then once more we were in open country, though here and there a golden acacia still flowered on the banks, so close to the water that Amara and Kathia, who were towing the canoe, had to stop and pass the rope round the water side of each. In an open space upon the bank, where no shrubs grew, we came upon a small herd of dun-coloured cattle, herded by two small girls in vivid cotton dresses. Every cow had her udder painted magenta, but one at the water's edge had been singled out for particular attention, for the most intimate part of her anatomy was dyed a gaudy cobalt blue. In close attendance upon her, and a little apart from the others, was the bull; his entire external sexual apparatus had been dyed to match. The cow wandered away from the herd and the bull snuffled after her; apart from the bright patch of colour on each they were dun-coloured against a dun landscape. The effect was more than grotesque, for their outlines merged into their neutral background, leaving only the blue portions substantial and significant, as bones show on a skeletal X-ray photograph; disembodied sexual organs out for a courting stroll on a fine spring morning. Thus must Adam and Eve have seemed to each other in the first awful moment after they had eaten of the fruit.

It conjured up great possibilities in my mind, this painting of whatever part of the body was of the greatest significance at the moment. It would be *dé rigueur* for guests at a banquet to come with blue mouths and hands; for the speaker at a lecture to have a blue mouth and his audience blue ears. Visitors to art gallery or theatre would have blue eyelids; every dowager as she bent to sniff a blossom at the Chelsea Flower Show would have a blue nose. . . . And yet on reflection it was frightening to think how many people and for how much of the time would look just like the bull and the cow.

Two hours later we turned into the Chahala, a broad placid river with a fringe of palms and reed houses at both banks, and spent the night at the stone fort of Sheikh Sadam. With two or three other sheikhs' homes I remember this place as unusual in that it was possible to stretch one's legs and walk, even wander for a short distance, molested neither by dogs nor by crowds. Between the fort and the river was a big grassy stretch, almost a lawn, where one could stroll in company with a scruffy-looking tame Sacred

Ibis, and even the towpath of the river itself was deserted and delectable for the greater part of the time.

At the darkening we went across the two-hundred-yard-wide river to a house of Sabians upon the opposite bank. The great majority of skilled work in Southern Iraq is done by Sabians, and we wanted two things repaired; Hassan had finally succeeded in breaking the fishing spear which had first broken my nose, and I had lost the chain ring from the end of a pocket knife to which I was particularly attached.

Even now there is still much to be discovered about the Sabians, though their communities extend far into accessible territory.

In all there are perhaps ten thousand Sabians in Iraq. Their name is that of a religion, not of a race, and it is neither Muslim nor Christian; though, together with those and the Jewish faith, Mahommed classed them as "People of the Book". Christ they look upon as a perverter of the truth, and he has no place in their religion, but John the Baptist they regard as a teacher of great wisdom, for they regard flowing water as the life-fluid, and with it are bound up all their elaborate rituals and customs. Thus they cannot live in the marshes, where the water is static, but on the rivers that surround them; and only the more secluded ones at that, for they seek privacy for their rites. (Once I told Thesiger of a cocktail party in London where in a momentary dead silence a voice went on loudly with the last words of a sentence. ". . . and only copulate at two o'clock in the morning, in running water." "Ah," said Thesiger, "Sabians"; but in fact the speaker had been describing some species of wildfowl.)

The Sabians, or *Subbi* as the Arabs call them—and the word has its root in the idea of immersion—have a script of their own, known only to their priests, and it is not uncommon to find fragments of pottery inscribed with their holy writings. Their religion has not spread beyond the frontiers of Iraq, and outside their own country they are known chiefly for their silverwork, a closely guarded process whose result has the appearance of a photograph reproduced on smooth silver.

The two Sabian craftsmen to whose house we went that night were father and son, and apart from the difference in their ages were as alike as Tweedledum and Tweedledee, with whom they had in common, also, a certain squat solidity. Both were very short men with full patriarchal beards, that of the father white and that of the son black; both had a certain nobleness and placidity of expression, and both wore wire-rimmed spectacles with completely circular eyepieces. They wore long white robes, European jackets, and the red check headcloth that in other parts of the Middle East distinguishes a Sunni from a Shi'a, but which in Iraq is worn only by the Sabians. The house which we entered was also the workshop, and against the matting wall between the reed arches lay a handful of tools and a varied collection of scrap metal. The old man began to work on my knife, and as I watched him I was reminded vividly of somebody else.

When I was a child my family had a gamekeeper whose hobby it was to work with small mechanical things, and for this he had a genius that might, had he been born into a different *milieu*, have made of him a great inventor. Nothing broken but Hannam could mend it, from a wrist-watch to the axle of a car; no engineering problem was of too complex invention for Hannam to overcome it. When I was sixteen he made for me the only really efficient silencer for a .22 rifle that I have ever seen, and I remember his telling me then that he had discovered how to make a total silencer for a shot-gun, but that he would never make the invention public because it would be murder. All this intricate work he carried out in a primitive shed which he had built from hammered-out oil cans. He was comparatively well equipped with the tools of his trade, but that he could handle them at all with those great horny hands was a perpetual miracle.

I remember his thumbs as having the general appearance and degree of mobility of the big toes of a giant who went habitually barefoot, and when he was working with soldering irons I have seen the smoke curling up from them and smelt the tang of singeing flesh while he was unaware of any discomfort. Between one of these thumbs and a correspondingly unsuitable forefinger he would try for long minutes at a time to pick up some tiny screw that eluded him, and to aid him in this seemingly impossible task he would adjust a pair of steel-rimmed spectacles, the very counterparts of those that the Sabians wore, whose enormously thick lenses showed that their function was not to correct the vision but only to magnify. The comparison was extraordinarily complete; the spectacles, the big horny inept-looking hands, the innate dignity of bearing and gentle courtesy of manner. In such a community Hannam would have been among kindred spirits, though he would have had little patience with the rituals of religion. One day the Minister of the kirk met him on the road and reproached him with his habitual failure in kirk attendance, but Hannam replied good-humouredly: "Na, na, Minister, we're the dodos, and we maunna fall oot wi' each other. The next generation will have no use for either your profession or mine."

Like Hannam, the Sabians were satisfied with no less than perfection in their work; and, also like Hannam, they would accept no payment for it, though this, I think, was in deference to Thesiger's reputation as a benign power.

Early next morning we went on down the Chahala, broad, slow-running, and dreamy, reflecting a blue sky on a pale satin surface and fringed at both banks with reed houses and scattered palms. There was a *mudhif* every few hundred yards; the sheikhs here were two a penny, or, as one of the canoe boys put it in characteristically vivid phrase, "each one in the fundamental orifice of the next." After an hour we stopped at the *mudhif* of Yunis ibn Hafudh, a villainous-looking young man whom I would have wanted neither as friend nor enemy. The *mudhif* was bright with cushions and carpets spread by numerous and very black slaves; the rugs laid near to the door in the places of honour were garish and gaudy with aniline dyes and crude designs, but farther back and hiding apologetically in the shadows were a pair of old and really magnificent carpets, each some twenty-five feet long and ten feet across. One was worn in places, but the other was perfect; I know little of rugs, but these I could see were certainly worth quite a few hundred pounds. Thesiger followed my gaze.

"Fine, aren't they? I've often noticed them. They don't value them at all; it's modern trash they like, and if they've got money that's what they furnish their houses with. Don't admire them or he'll give them to us, and it would be embarrassing—I never accept presents in the marshes."

The talk, for some reason that I forget, turned on birds, and here was another astounding example of the superstitions filling the heads even of wealthy people like these who not infrequently visited the big westernised cities. Yunis questioned us quite seriously as to the existence and geographical location of the bird who can carry away the roc who is carrying away an elephant. How simple and exciting life would be, I thought, if one could seek these miracles in the external sensory world without recourse to the dismaying miracles of science or where the human mind has cliffs of fall, frightful, sheer.

After a time the talk turned on a matter that I could not understand, and I began to look out through the *mudhif* entrance. A tame gazelle grazed some thirty yards away; on the opposite bank of the river a strikingly beautiful little girl was pasting dough into the inside of a conical mud oven. Her features were almost perfect, and unadorned by any tattooing; the regularity of the bone structure in itself would have been beautiful without the addition of those glorious eyes, the golden skin, and the blue sheen on the flow of her straight hair that fell like a dark sheet of falling water to her shoulders, without the delicate lips and the expression that still held the sweetness of childhood. She was, I thought, the most beautiful child I had ever seen; then, as she straightened from the oven, her bright blue cotton dress outlined her small high breasts, and I realised that to these people she was not a child, and was in fact almost marriageable. She might have been twelve years old, but small for that age.

Sabeti, sitting at my shoulder, had noticed my absorption. "Helu, Gavin?" he whispered, nudging me, "t'arid?" "Na-am, helu," I replied coldly. The image of that superb little creature in the arms of some loutish Ma'dan was not wholly pleasing.

Nearer to hand, just outside the entrance of the *mudhif*, a large reddish-coloured sheep, uncouth and comfortable-looking, lay munching with gusto from a pile of cut green *hashish*. Someone, a child perhaps, had twined a blue ribbon in the wool of her neck. She chewed the cud with her mouth open, and belched more than once; she appeared to enjoy what she was doing very much. As I watched her a man came round the corner of the *mudhif* carrying unsheathed a big curved knife. He grasped the sheep by the wool of her neck and dragged her protesting but still munching out of my line of vision. Thesiger had told me that this was a hospitable household who would probably kill a sheep for us; somehow it seemed to me unthinkable to eat that preposterous old harridan with her oafish and confiding ways, and that if I were required to swallow one mouthful of her I should be sick. She would still be munching as the knife slit her throat, and then she would die very slowly until at last she was choked by her own blood, and the blue ribbon would be sodden with it. Thesiger was unsentimental about animals, so I kept my thoughts to myself, and ten minutes later the man with the knife reappeared, carrying under his arm a huge pile of freshly cut *hashish*. At his heels trotted the egregious ewe, marvellously intact, uncouth and voracious as ever; in a kneeling attitude she began immediately upon the replenishment to her larder which was set before her.

Our evening meal, however, was ruthlessly chased to a standstill before our eyes, but tasted none the worse for it. We had gone on a mile or so down the river to Mutashar, part of a straggling ribbon development on banks that were now of drab mud, unrelieved by any growth. There was much traffic on the river here, big dhows with forty-foot masts, whose full sails did little more in the still thundery air than counteract the river's current against them, so that the labouring men on the towpath, grotesquely naked from the waist downward made no more than some two miles an hour. Then the rain came, and the surface of packed mud between the houses became in a moment a puddled expanse of slippery clay. Here, still outside the marshes, there were no reeds to be thrown down as sand is thrown on any icy road in an English winter, and in a few minutes patches of water had formed, into which the big drops of the thunder shower splashed and sizzled.

The rain stopped as suddenly as it had begun, but it left an interesting terrain for the capture of our dinner. With the end of the shower poultry had come out from the shelter of their owners' houses, and were regarding with obvious discontent the unscratchable surface around them. We were sitting in a *mudhif* from which the covering reed matting had been rolled up for the first four feet all round, so that the overhead structure formed a canopy, as it were, leaving unimpeded vision on all sides. Our host called a boy to him and indicated a splendid and extremely inedible-looking cock who picked his way majestically among the puddles. He was a very remarkable bird, and would have commanded more than passing attention in any farmyard.

He had the vivid colouring of the wild Indian jungle fowl, more familiar to most people now through nineteenth-century prints of cock-fighting, but he was as big as a Rhode Island Red and his spurs were four inches long.

The boy beckoned another, and the two of them began to close in upon this gaudy fowl with cautious squelches through the mud. He realised their intention at once, and early lost his dignity, his steps becoming short and uncertain, his neck craning from side to side in little nervous jerks. At length he undertook a flurried rush, his fright bursting from his throat in staccato hysteria. One of the two boys bounded to cut him off, slid, and came down on his face in the mud. By the time he had recovered himself the cock, with the second boy hard on his heels, had disappeared round the corner of a house. The hunt was out of our sight for perhaps a minute, though a swelling babel of shrill cries told that the cock was holding off the challenge. At length he shot into view again, leading by a full ten yards a rabble of a dozen or more children of all ages armed with sticks or reeds, splashed from head to foot with mud, and skidding in wild pandemonium at every corner. A girl dashed out from her house trying to head the quarry, lost her footing and went over on her face with her sole garment round her shoulders and her round golden posteriors bare to the sky. Round and round, in and out among the houses laboured the panting procession, the cock still holding his lead and the pack behind him growing every minute. At length two or three pi-dogs, gradually stirred by the commotion out of their flea-scratching lethargy, began to harass the fugitive in a half-hearted sort of way from the flanks and the front; and the cock, now panting and exhausted, suddenly sought sanctuary. It was a cruel chance that he sought it in the heart of the enemy camp. The pack was out of sight behind him as for perhaps the twentieth time he legged it across the open space outside our *mudhif*, and, outflanked by a yapping cur, he made a sudden dive for its shelter. He stood among us in the half light within, gasping but quite motionless, the splendid green plumage of his tail trembling lightly. I would have accorded him the sanctuary that the dim light and the arches seemed to demand, for even the humblest *mudhif* is a little like a cathedral, but our host leant over with a laugh and scooped him up; he left the *mudhif* with the cock in one hand, swinging by the legs, and a curved marshman's knife in the other.

At Mutashar we were near to the edge of the permanent marsh again, and only a few miles from Dibin. Someone in the *mudhif* had recently returned from there, and told us that three days ago the eagle owl had been alive and well. We reached Dibin the next evening, and as the permanent marsh closed round us again, greener, denser, and more confined than it had been three weeks before, I realised that I welcomed it, and that some part of me had fretted for it during our stay among the cultivating people. I could have made the marshes my home, but never the unfriendly wastes of mud and irrigating channels that surrounded them.

We went to the *mudhif*. The scene had changed much since we were last here; Dibin seemed no longer a mud island in a great lake on whose surface grew scattered and withered sedge, for the new verdure of soft and bending reed leaves grew everywhere to within a stone's throw of the houses, and a few hundred yards away, where the passage of boats had not hindered their growth, a canoe and its standing occupant became quickly hidden among them.

No one referred to the eagle owl, and after a little time I inquired for it. I thought the people looked a little furtively at each other. It was not well, they said, had not been well for two days. They brought it to me. Those three weeks since I had seen it had made the changes that as many months would have made for a human prisoner in Buchenwald or Belsen. There was no flesh at all upon the breast, and the great blade of the bone stood out like a knife through the feathers. The feathers were coated with hardened slime and filth, and someone had pulled its tail out; one eye was inflamed and partially closed. Its crop, however, was full, and bulging with some soft squashy matter. It had grown dark in the *mudhif*, and I carried the bird out of the circle of the firelight and set it down in the deep shadows between the feet of the farther arch columns. I was angry for the humiliation of something beautiful and savage, angry as I would be for these people themselves when they became humiliated by the soiling contact of our modern civilisation. They felt none of this, any more than the people of the oil-fields felt it for the tribesmen who drifted in to them and put off their *dish-dashas* for soiled and shoddy western clothes, their primitive convictions for soiled and shoddy western ideas that fitted no better than their shabby suits. The sight of all humiliation is unbearable to me, and I have often regretted my ready ability to identify myself with animals as well as humans, bringing as it does a sharing of too much misery.

I came back to the circle and asked what they had given the bird to eat. What I had told them, they said; a few birds, bats from the roof of the *mudhif*, and sometimes a little fish. Then I asked what its crop was full of at the moment. Thesiger did the translation for me, and he was infected a little by my anger, for he had a feeling for creatures of prey. They said they did not know, for the woman of the *mudhif* had fed it that day. I went back to the owl with a torch. It had brought up the contents of its crop, and was very obviously dying. At first I thought that it was some kind of meat that lay on the ground beside it in the dim light of the torch. Then I saw what it really was; it was date pulp. The woman came into the *mudhif* just then, and I went back to the fire and told Thesiger about the dates. Thus driven into a corner this shocking female confessed unashamedly to having forcibly fed that great bird of prey first with whole slabs of doughy Arab bread and then, when it looked rather unwell as a result, with a mush of pulped dates. Probably it had never had a morsel of flesh since we left Dibin. "And I suppose," Thesiger concluded a summary of her mental powers "that if you had a captive lion you would feed it on grapes and *hashish*."

The great bird died a few hours later, draggled and contorted. Poor humiliated eagle of the silent glittering night, wings clipped, tail pulled out, stuffed with bread and dates until it died squalidly on the ground, stained with its own excrement, in a dim corner of its captors' dwelling, one great orange eye still open and staring out to the stars.

I brooded over the owl. Part of my tension, I recognised, was due to the removal from me of a promised shred of responsibility; I should have had the well-being of a living creature to care for, a little outlet for my restless and frustrated energy, an object for the desire to protect something that is always strong in me. I felt an unreasonable hatred for that witless woman with her show of bustle and competence, and contempt that even her avarice had not mastered her stupidity. Thinking of these things, I was not trying to understand the conversation around me when the words *"celb mai"* caught my ear. "What was that about otters?" I asked Thesiger.

"I think we've got you that otter cub you said you wanted. This fellow comes from that village half a mile away; he says he's had one for about ten days. Very small and sucks milk from a bottle. Do you want it?"

I said, "It sounds exactly what I wanted, but I think we'd better not say anything definite. It might be the owl over again; probably they've been giving it methylated spirits."

The otter's owner said he would fetch it and be back in half an hour or so. He got up and went out; through the entrance of the *mudhif* I could see his canoe glide away silently over the star-reflecting water.

Presently he returned carrying the cub, came across into the firelight and put it down on my knee as I sat cross-legged. It looked up and chittered at me gently. It was the size of a kitten or a squirrel, still a little unsteady on its legs, with a stiff-looking tapering tail the length of a pencil, and it exhaled a wholly delightful malty smell. It rolled over on its back, displaying a round furry stomach and the soles of four webbed feet.

"Well," said Thesiger, "do you want her?" I nodded. "How much are you prepared to pay for her?"

"Certainly more than they would ask."

"I'm not going to pay some ridiculous price—it's bad for prestige. We'll take her if they'll sell her for a reasonable price; if not, we'll get one somewhere else."

I said, "Let's make certain of getting this one; we're near the end of the time now, and we may not get another chance. And after all the prestige doesn't matter so much as this is your last visit to the marshes." I saw this fascinating little creature eluding me for the sake of a few shillings' worth of prestige, and the negotiations seemed to me interminable.

In the end we bought the cub for five dinar, the price to include the rubber teat and the filthy but precious bottle from which she was accustomed to drink. Bottles are a rarity in the marshes.

Most infant animals are engaging, but this cub had more charm per cubic inch of her tiny body than all the young animals I had ever seen. Even now I cannot write about her without a pang.

I cut a collar for her from the strap of my field-glasses— a difficult thing, for her head was no wider than her neck— and tied six foot of string to this so as to retain some permanent contact with her if at any time she wandered away from me. Then I slipped her inside my shirt, and she snuggled down at once in a security of warmth and darkness that she had not known since she was reft from her mother. I carried her like that through her short life;

when she was awake her head would peer wonderingly out from the top of the pullover, like a kangaroo from its mother's pouch, and when she was asleep she slept as otters like to, on her back with her webbed feet in the air. When she was awake her voice was a bird-like chirp, but in her dreams she would give a wild little cry on three falling notes, poignant and desolate. I called her Chahala, after the river we had left the day before, and because those syllables were the nearest one could write to the sound of her sleeping cry.

I slept fitfully that night; all the pi-dogs of Dibin seemed to bark at my ears, and I dared not in any case let myself fall into too sound a sleep lest I should crush Chahala, who now snuggled in my armpit. Like all otters, she was "house-trained" from the beginning, and I had made things easy for her by laying my sleeping bag against the wall of the *mudhif*, so that she could step straight out on the patch of bare earth between the reed columns. This she did at intervals during the night, backing into the very farthest corner to produce, with an expression of infinite concentration, a tiny yellow caterpillar of excrement. Having inspected this, with evident satisfaction at a job well done, she would clamber up my shoulder and chitter gently for her bottle. This she preferred to drink lying on her back and holding the bottle between her paws as do bear cubs, and when she had finished sucking she would fall sound asleep with the teat still in her mouth and a beatific expression on her baby face.

She accepted me as her parent from the moment that she first fell asleep inside my pullover, and never once did she show fear of anything or anyone, but it was as a parent that I failed her, for I had neither the knowledge nor the instinct of her mother, and when she died it was because of my ignorance. Meanwhile this tragedy, so small but so complete, threw no shadow on her brief life, and as the days went by she learned to know her name and to play a little as a kitten does, and to come scuttling along at my heels if I could find dry land to walk on, for she hated to get her feet wet. When she had had enough of walking she would chirp and paw at my legs until I squatted down so that she could climb up and dive head first into the friendly darkness inside my pullover; sometimes she would at once fall asleep in that position, head downward with the tip of her pointed tail sticking out at the top. The Arabs called her my daughter, and used to ask me when I had last given her suck.

I found myself missing Chahala as I wrote of her, so I set down my manuscript book and pen and went to the open door and whistled, and out of the sea fifty yards away came Mijbil, Chahala's successor, and galloped up over the sand and pranced round me like a puppy, and then came in with me and went to sleep on his back on the hearthrug. Mijbil was a very important otter, of a race quite new to science, and that discovery might never have been made if Chahala had not died; but still I think I would rather she had lived and *Lutrogale perspicillata maxwelli* had remained incognito, for in assuming my name and remaining my constant companion for a year he took too much of my heart.

We left Dibin next morning, through a country filled with a bewildering host of migrating birds, and spent that night at the *mudhif* of Haji Mahaisin, on the Agra. A few hundred yards from us, on the main waterway at right angles to ours, stood the imposing fortress of Nasr of evil repute. For some years past he had been strengthening it, so that now it appeared impregnable to men armed only with small arms. The compound was heavily encircled with barbed wire, and against a flame-coloured sunset the silhouettes of armed slaves showed where look-outs had been posted at various points on the wall of the fort itself. The government had established a precautionary police post hard by the wall of the compound, and police sentries with sub-machine-guns patrolled the entrance from the river front and stood guard over the big white motor launch that was tied up there. I should not have cared to have joined his brother Jabir in an attack on that fort.

I soon found that the cub Chahala was restrictive of movement and activity. Carried habitually inside my pullover, she made an enceinte-looking bulge which collected the whole village round me as soon as I set foot outside the door; furthermore I could no longer carry my camera round my neck as I did normally, for it bumped against her body as I walked.

We moved in short journeys; the next day, I remember, we lunched at a village where there was a malarial epidemic, and there was not enough Paludrine left in our stocks to treat a tenth of the people who required it. That night we reached the fort of Talib, half-brother of Nasr and Jabir, who as a boy had opened fire on the Sayid deputy whom their grandfather, old Salman, had sent to reason with him when he rose in protest against the favouritism shown to Nasr. We did not stay there, however, for Talib turned out to be away in Amara, being tried for the alleged rape of a merchant's daughter, a trial from which he eventually escaped with a petty fine. No one seemed to have the keys of the fort, so we stayed at the *mudhif* of Sayid Qadhim nearby.

That evening Thesiger and I discussed the prospect of weaning Chahala. We both felt that she should be old enough to eat solid food, and I felt that her rather skinny little body would benefit by something stronger than buffalo milk. However, I underestimated the power of instinct, for I thought that she would not connect flesh or blood with edibility and would need to be introduced to the idea very gradually. The best way to do this, I decided, was to introduce a few drops of blood into her milk to get her used to the taste. This proved to be extraordinarily naïve, for while I was holding the bodies of two decapitated sparrows and trying to drip a little blood from them into her feeding bottle she suddenly caught the scent of the red meat and made a savage grab for the carcasses. I think that if I had not stopped her she would have crunched up bone and all with those tiny needle-like teeth, and we took this as evidence that she had already been introduced by her mother to adult food. I took the carcasses from her, much to her evident fury; and when I gave her the flesh from the breasts cut up small she wolfed it down savagely and went questing round for more.

"Finish with milk" said Amara with a gesture of finality, "finish, finish; she is grown up now." And it seemed so, but, alas, she was not.

The next night we spent at the *mudhif* of a somewhat unusual sheikh. He was a young man in his middle twenties, and one of the only two feminine-type homosexuals that I saw in the marshes. It is true that the marshmen, in common with many other Arab peoples, are not very selective in their direction of sexual outlet; all is, so to speak, grist to their mill, and the long years that many a youth of the poorer people may have to wait before he has acquired the bride-price of three buffaloes, coupled with the tremendous taboos attached to intercourse with a girl of the village, make casual homosexuality general. It is not, however, the outcome of any exclusive leaning in that direction, and no shame is attached to it; I have heard young married men discuss quite openly whether they would rather sleep with their wives or with some particular boy, and usually reach the conclusion, after some argument, that they would prefer their wives. This sheikh, however, was something quite different; he was the feminine type that in England would be described as a pansy. He wore a *dish-dasha* of bright sky-blue, a pale beautifully cut European jacket, white buckskin shoes, two symmetrically placed gold teeth, and, surprisingly, a wide eyebrow-moustache. The little finger of his right hand was dyed with henna to the middle joint, and on the finger next to it he wore two heavy gold rings, one set with diamonds and the other with a single sapphire. From his shoulders floated a diaphanous blue gauze *bisht* edged with rich gold embroidery.

He received us not in a *mudhif* but a *sarifa*, the small rectangular and often ornate reed house which many sheikhs maintain to entertain their personal friends in an atmosphere more *intime* than that of the *mudhif*. This *sarifa* was richly furnished in execrable European taste; the sofas and chairs were of the same type, mass produced in Basra and Baghdad, as are to be found in every sheikh's reception room, but their upholstery was more flamboyant, an imitation velvet brocade with a pattern of big white fleur-de-lis on a blue ground. A heavy modern silk carpet covered the floor, in whose riotous pattern a heavily laden camel could be distinguished mistrustfully inspecting a group of chamoix on a nearby alpine peak, while farther off something that could be none other than a moose gazed with obvious dismay into the veiled face of a Tuareg who was menacing it with what appeared to be a sub-machine-gun. In the extreme foreground a green parakeet preened itself oblivious of its ecological insecurity.

The sheikh's fancy fell on Sabeti, who squirmed with embarrassment, and, I think, pleasure. Probably he had never been ogled like this before, for he was a very plain young man with a big nose and an habitual air of apology. The sheikh draped himself on the arm of a chair and chattered and ate nuts from a little leather bag and flashed his gold teeth, and Sabeti sat cross-legged on the floor and gazed up with a moonstruck face that would undoubtedly have infuriated his wife.

I saw only one other womanish man in the marshes, and he was an extreme case, a transvestist. He was a robustly built man with no physical abnormality, who dressed as a woman, lived with the women, and did woman's work. He followed us about for some time, requesting us to perform a surgical operation that would make him a complete woman —a formidable task indeed, for he was at the moment a very complete man. Thesiger told me that the comparable situation among women was not rare, some women assuming a complete masculine role and dressing as men, and that these were approved by the men as being a stage in advance of normal womanhood.

Presently the sheikh left the *sarifa* in company with a muscular Ethiopian slave, who, I was told, was one of his stud of stallions, employed at a nightly fee which another slave confided to our crew, and which seemed wholly inadequate for the work.

That night was one of the few, during the whole journey, that I passed in acute discomfort. The *sarifa* was partially open at ground level, and over the zoological fantasy of the silk carpet tore an icy wind which only the chamoix could have endured with equanimity. It was bitter, and it blew all night. Thesiger and the others were rolled tightly in their blankets, but I had to leave the side of my sleeping bag open to allow exit to Chahala, who sensibly took shelter in the warmth behind my body. I lay shivering and listening to the jackals howling in the distance. I remember that a slant of weak moonlight came through the lattice and fell on Amara's face; he was sleeping with his lips drawn back from his teeth to the gums, an expression of hatred so intense and yet so static as to appear inhuman.

During the slow icy hours between midnight and dawn, hours when the brain may sometimes outrun the plodding of reason and escape from habitual and safe corridors of thought to catch perilous glimpses of truth, some part of me was trying to interpret and give meaning to my presence here in the night and the cold on the bank of a strange river. I tried to think of the name of the place where I was, but I found that I did not know it, nor could I now project a map in my mind. I turned, and my eyes came back to the grinning mask of Amara's face in the moonlight. I must be here for some purpose, I thought, for those who wake at night in desert and in jungle to see the stars at strange slants in the sky have some goal before them, some enemy to conquer before returning home. The lines that drew them here would form some plan on paper, a firm design that showed the growth and aim of their endeavour, a geometry that expressed the journey of their lives. I tried to see my own like this and saw it as a doodle on a scrap of paper beside a telephone, formless, full of heraldic flourishes and ignoble retreat, with here and there a random line running far out on to the blank page; and at the end of one of these I lay now listening to the jackals skirling at the moon. What went ye forth for to see? A reed shaken by the wind?

In the morning we made a very short journey to the *mudhif* of Sheikh Jabir, whom three weeks before we had met at Dibin preparing to make war on his brother Nasr. The *mudhif* was on the bank of a narrow watercourse with land on one side of it and palms in the distance, a humble and untidy building speaking of poverty in striking contrast with the aggresive fortress of Nasr. He seemed a different man now from him who had led the war dance at Dibin, for though the issue was still in doubt it was rumoured that things were not going well for Nasr in Baghdad, and that the government would give a decision against him. Jabir had lost the wolfish and distrustful expression that he had worn when he was raising the tribesmen; he seemed assured and confident now, and he greeted us with great courtesy and friendliness.

We went out in the afternoon to shoot pig, and as we left the *mudhif* with Jabir in the *tarada* with us a passing canoe hailed him.

"There is news from Baghdad—Nasr is finished! Allah be praised!"

"Allah be praised," replied Jabir quietly. He said nothing else, nor did he refer to the subject again, but his mind must have been full of it, for his whole future had changed. Before, he had been a sheikh only in name; now he would have money and lands and position and many of the army of slaves that had belonged to Nasr. I thought of Nasr's future, and because I did not know him and his vices were nothing to me I could pity him. He would be a hunted man now, a fugitive, without friends or money or property; driven perhaps like Aboud who had killed Dakhil in the shooting accident, to live beside a police post in the country of his enemies, until one day the police protection would not be enough, and his body would be found in a muddy channel.

I remember that afternoon particularly for the splendour of the sky. Against a background of the deepest blue great elongated cotton-wool clouds fanned out over us like the fingers of a giant hand; they seemed as solid a structure as the banks of the watercourse or the high prow of the *tarada*. We went downstream through idyllic palm groves with blossoming acacias and willows and the spring of delicate new grass, and on into recently inundated land, where the reeds were thin and short and green. The whole air here was a jewelled kaleidoscope of colour; a myriad bee-eaters thronged the reeds and the air above them, each one of this horde as gorgeous as any humming-bird. They darted low over the water with glittering glint of electric green, soared up to show the blinding sheen of copper beneath their wings, alighted in gemlike array upon the reeds that bent to the water under their weight. It was as though a rainbow had suddenly come to pieces and filled the air with irresponsible fragments.

Chahala slept in my pullover, and because of her I remained in the *tarada* with Jabir when Thesiger waded off to hunt for pig. It was impossible to be bored with so much to look at. Scattered pelicans drifted on the water, immobile as stuffed birds; overhead wheeled a restless pack of some five hundred clamorous stilts, a weird urgent clangour something between the calling of wild geese and of seagulls, haunting and unfamiliar as the tang of a strange spice.

Among the copper iridescence of the bee-eaters' wings the kingfishers flitted, halcyons of chestnut and blinding blue, and pied kingfisher of staccato black-and-white; they hovered with their bodies held upright in the air, and their heads, below the vibrating wings, craned intently downward to peer into the water; they dived swift and arrow-like in a vertical plunge. Against the blue sky the pale bulrush tops looked like raw wool on the spindle of an old spinning-wheel, and above them flew, with the infinitely slow wing-beat of a giant, a single Goliath heron, a bird that stands nearly as high as a man.

We went home in the evening to Jabir's *mudhif*, through waterways only a few paces across and with hard banks at their sides. The canoe boys were infected by the glory of the evening, and towed the *tarada* as fast as they could run, so that the thrust of the long craft in the narrow channel piled at our sides smooth rushing walls of water that were blood-coloured with the stain of the sinking sun. From the banks ahead of us yard-wide soft-shelled terrapins, or mud-turtles, plopped into the water in noisy panic.

Night had come before we reached the *mudhif*, and the moon was like a marshman's curved dagger lying bright on dark velvet.

We travelled the next morning to a *mudhif* belonging to one of Jabir's brothers. He had not, it seemed, suffered as badly at the hands of his misguided father as had Jabir, for it was a noble building, on the bank of a broad, brimming river, and it appeared the fresher and better tended for the sprigs of green corn-stem that decorated the arches in recognition of the New Year. The reed matting skirt of the wall next to the river had been furled up to allow entry to the cool breeze, and from where I sat I watched for more than two hours a monstrous profligacy of nature; a squander-ing, a wastage so gigantic that the thought of numbers became as meaningless as when the brain tries to embrace the concept of the Milky Way. The river water flowed past the *mudhif* at some five or six miles an hour, and it was sixty yards across, yet during all of the two hours hardly a square foot of that smoothly sliding surface was bare to the sky. As the static waterways of the marshes were blanketed by a dense layer of white-and-gold flowers, so this river carried a great moving carpet of a myriad shivering, dying insect wings. Somewhere, perhaps far up the river's course, these delicate gauze-winged creatures, in appearance something between a dragonfly and a mayfly, had hatched in their unthinkable millions, and sailed down the river, drowning as they drifted, to form this stupendous funereal pageant.

We came in the evening to a big *mudhif* at a point where three waterways joined, with dry land on all sides and, here and there, thinly scattered palm groves. We were greeted by a slave on the bank who led us into the *mudhif* and went in search of his master. There was only one man there when we entered; he was seated cross-legged against the right-hand wall, and he did not rise nor audibly acknowledge our greeting. There was little of his face visible, for he wore his *agal* muffled round his face and mouth as though he had toothache. We sat down opposite to him, and he remained quite motionless, watching us with black eyes that seemed totally expressionless. He was, as far as one could see, a young man, tall and well-built, certainly not a *haji*, who would be most likely to express disapproval of our presence in this way. I tried returning his stare, but he did not look away.

"A singularly bloody-minded young man," said Thesiger after a while. "Probably another Sayid who is going to harangue the company about the degradation of eating with Christians; though if he feels like that about it I can't understand why he doesn't go. A trouble-maker; you'll see."

Presently the sheikh arrived, and gradually the *mudhif* began to fill up, and after an hour there were some thirty or forty people all chattering away, but still the muffled figure sat quite silent. We ate, but he did not eat with us, nor did he chide anyone else for doing so.

Thesiger said, "Can't understand it. He's holding his fire; he's up to no good, that's one thing that's quite certain."

Another hour passed and at last we said that we were tired and wanted to sleep. The company rose and began to file out, but still the figure opposite to us remained quite motionless. If anything the intensity of the stare increased. A slave came up and muttered to Thesiger, who turned to me.

"He's wounded—pig got him in the face. He's been waiting all this time to ask if we can do anything for him. We maligned him." He signalled to the man, who came diffidently across to him.

Under the *agal* his face and head were swathed in rag bandages that were stiff and brown with dried blood. They separated with difficulty, and as I watched the man's eyes I could see now that he was in great pain.

The wounds were appalling. Something had driven clean through his cheek, smashing the teeth of both upper and lower jaw and tearing the tongue; moreover this great hole in the left side of his face gaped as if flesh were missing, and could not be drawn together. On the right side was another smaller wound in whose edges were embedded fragments of broken molar; there were other ragged punctures below the jaw bone on the left side, one of which had narrowly missed the jugular vein, and still another an inch below the eye. His left hand and wrist, too, seemed a lump of macerated flesh.

He had been in the bows of a canoe, we were told, which had run right on to the top of a pig sleeping in a reed thicket. The canoe had been overset, tipping him into the shallow water, and the pig had inflicted this fearful damage in a matter of seconds.

Thesiger did what he could. "And now," he said, turning to me, "you know what almost happened to you. Perhaps you won't be so offhand about it next time."

Because I did identify myself with this man, my own cheeks with this face that looked like a burst sausage in a frying pan, I was anxious for every detail of what had happened, but I could learn little more. He had thrown up his left hand to save his face—his right arm was underneath him—and the tusk had driven through his cheek and teeth into his mouth. That was all; I reflected that it was unreasonable to expect him to remember the minute details of a shattering assault that had lasted only seconds. But I could not visualise the scene; I could not see how the tusk of any ordinary boar could drive completely through the face so that it came out through the farther cheek, for the tusk lies close to the boar's snout, and is a weapon of sabre-slash rather than foil thrust. There, anyway, but for the grace. . . .

We did not see the man again in the morning, and I had stopped puzzling about his wounds by the time we left, rather earlier than usual, in order to avoid the visit on official business of the Provincial Governor's deputy. We travelled for some three hours, the watercourses giving place to marsh again, low and green, with every inch of open water choked with a dazzling and sweet-smelling blanket of white water buttercup. Sometimes there were whole lagoons of it, acres and acres of white, more dazzling under the sun than a mountain snowfield. I remember a corner of one of those lagoons, where above the white and golden flowers two brilliant halcyon kingfishers perched on a bent reed, and low overhead flew an osprey with heavily labouring wings, a great fish held in the stiff down-stretched clutch of its talons.

At about midday we came to a tiny village on a low island; there were only four houses upon it, and a hundred yards away across the water stood a fifth, farther away from the community than the marshmen usually like to build. We ate in the open air against the side of a house facing across to this single dwelling, eating roast—or, more aptly, burnt—coots that we had shot on the way. Chahala, the otter cub, pottered about in the rustling dry reeds at the house side and avidly bolted shreds of meat from the coots. After a time I noticed that the isolated house opposite to us seemed untenanted; there was no canoe tied up beside it, nor any sign of livestock, though on the buffalo platform was a pile of cut *hashish* that was just beginning to turn brown in the sun.

Our host confirmed that the house was empty; it had been deserted two days ago. The people who had lived in it were at odds with their sheikh, some question of unpaid dues, and the sheikh had sent an expedition to take reprisals. This expedition took the form of a small party of men who were to raid the house at night and remove everything of value that the householder possessed. They had come in a canoe about the middle of the night, a party of four men, and no one had woken when they entered. They were in the act of carrying out the wooden chest in which a marshman keeps the family's possessions when the householder had awoken. He sprang up, and seizing his fishing spear which stood against the wall beside him he had hurled it with all his strength at the head of the nearest figure. The five-pointed spear struck his face, he screamed and fell with the ten-foot shaft of the spear sticking up from his head. By now the rest of the little village was awake, dogs were barking, and men were calling across the water. The raiders dragged the wounded man into their canoe and made off into the night; the village could still hear his screams and groans when the canoe was far off in the darkness. The chest lay where the raiding party had dropped it, just inside the door of the house.

The householder, however, was in a state of panic. He had seen the shaft of the spear sticking out from the man's head as he lay upon the ground, and he was convinced that he had inflicted a mortal wound. He would be the object not only of terrible reprisals from his sheikh, but of a blood feud with his victim's family. There and then he had packed his few belongings into his canoe, and towing his water buffaloes behind them he and his family had fled in the opposite direction from that taken by the sheikh's men.

Thesiger asked quickly where the raiding party had come from, and was told the name of the village where we had stayed the night before.

"No wonder they seemed odd wounds for a pig to have made," he said; "that man had a whole fishing spear through his face. They must have cut it out with a knife; that's why there were great holes with flesh missing from them. I don't wonder he looked a bit old-fashioned at us."

I tried to remember the wounds in detail, and realised how lucky he had been. The centre prong of the five is nearly double the length of the flanking ones, and it had only been the fact of this longest point striking the molars at the far side of his jaw that had prevented the shorter ones penetrating his throat below and his eye above; I remembered the shallow punctures above the cheekbone and below the jawline. His right hand must have been carrying the chest, and he had thrown up his left in a last-moment attempt to protect his face as he saw the spear in the air. Those were the lacerations at his wrist and between his forefinger and thumb.

Thesiger looked moody; no one likes being deceived.

That night we spent at a large village of the Nuafa, a section of the Abu Mahommed tribe. It was a dense, crowded village on a low mud island, and we stayed at a house well back from the water, so that to reach it one ran the gauntlet of many pi-dogs who gave us slow calculating and uncanine stares as we passed. Our host was absent on a pilgrimage, and his son greeted us, a shifty-looking stripling of eighteen or so who did not seem particularly pleased to see us. We handed over to him our canoe poles and baggage for safe keeping with some ceremony. Thesiger said "You want to watch these people. They've got no sheikh, haven't had one for three months—an experiment of the government. That means they're not answerable to any immediate authority they're scared of, which is always a bad thing with these people."

Chahala, the otter cub, attracted the usual amount of attention, and presently a boy brought two wagtails for her to eat. He had pulled out the long feathers of their wings, and they lay there helpless in his hands, their eyes bright with terror and the tiny bodies shaken by the hammering of their hearts. He had caught them, he said, in a miniature model of the big clap-nets in which on the cultivating land surrounding the marshes duck are caught. He caught several small birds every day, "to play with". I knew by now what that would mean among these people; the wing feathers would be pulled out as these were, and a child would drag the bird about with a string tied to its leg until he got tired of it, when a cat would take up the sport where he had left off. The boy was proud of his skill; he looked at us with soft eyes in a gentle flower-like face, and offered to show us his net. One could no more be angry with him than one could reproach any beautiful little beast of prey. Thesiger spoke my own thoughts. "It's no use getting worked up about it; these people are what they are, and animal suffering means nothing to them. You can't let these go anyway, he's pulled the wing feathers out."

He took them and pressed his thumb over their hearts, and with a little shivering flutter they were dead. Chahala ate the meat from their breasts, and she was as beautiful as they, though it was her last day of life. Later that evening we shot a buff-backed heron for her, and she wolfed the shredded flesh avidly. It was the last food that she ate.

It was very cold that night. Over my head was a gap in the reed matting of the roof through which the stars showed bright and unobscured, but a thin wind that seemed as chill as the tinkle of icicles rustled the dry reeds at the foot of the wall, and I slept fitfully. Chahala was restless and would not stay still in my sleeping bag; I did not know that she was dying, and I was impatient with her. All night there was movement about the low fire beyond the reed platform at the centre of the house, and once I woke to see the youth who was our host standing naked on the platform and apparently rearranging the bundle of canoe poles that was propped against it; but I had forgotten what Thesiger had said, and I thought nothing of it.

In the morning I took Chahala to a spit of dry land beyond the edge of the village to let her walk, and only then I realised that she was very ill. She would not move, but lay looking up at me pathetically, and when I picked her up again she instantly sought the warm darkness inside my pullover.

I wanted to tell Thesiger about this, but when I came back to the houses he was surrounded by a great crowd of people all talking and shouting at once, and I could not get near him. There was nothing very strange about this; the surgery hour often got out of hand and assumed much this appearance. I did not understand that this was an angry crowd—I had noticed before how like the expression of one emotion among these people was to another—and I thought nothing of it. By this time I could sometimes follow the gist of a conversation in Arabic, though I spoke little, but no individual words were distinguishable in that babel of voices. I wandered away again, reassuring myself that Chahala was no worse than when Sheikh Jabir had given her mutton, and that she would recover. The village seemed half empty now that so many people were gathered round Thesiger, and I used the unwonted peace to take photographs less handicapped than usually. The prows of rows of canoes at the edge of the water were reflected as a pattern of black downturned claws, and above them on the blue sky were strange white clouds that faithfully repeated the design.

But the pathos of small and helpless deaths seemed everywhere that morning. Near the water's edge toddled a brood of wild goslings that had been reared under a hen. A black and white crow came and perched on the prow of a canoe near by, and cocked his head at them with a cold bright eye and a bill like the black blade of a commando knife. The hen clucked fussily and began to lead her brood away from the water, but one was farther away than the others, and as he hurried after her with a forward-leaning run there was a clop of black wings overhead and the crow was on him. The crow killed him very slowly, allowing him to escape apparently unhurt several times and hurry cheeping pitifully after the hen. It was after the third time this had happened that I saw the gosling now had only one eye. He was still living when the crow carried him off across the water, the small webbed feet feebly paddling the air. And not a sparrow falls. . . . How very heavy, I thought, must be the heart of the Creator.

When I approached the crowd again Thesiger was forcing his way through it, and shouting to make himself heard. I remember that at his elbow a woman gesticulated furiously and screamed out what could only be abuse; balanced on her head was a full basket of buffalo dung from which not a fragment fell. Thesiger strode through the villagers like a giant among pygmies.

"Dogs!" he was shouting, "dogs, and sons of black dogs! Black dogs and children of pigs!" In the background I could see our canoe boys carrying our baggage down to the *tarada*. Thesiger was so angry that he could spare few words of English explanation to interrupt his rich flow of rhetoric. "Stole our things in the night, that boy who was our host . . . all in on it, the whole village. . . . " We reached the *tarada*, and as we pushed off he stood up in the bows and went on rebuking the hostile crowd on the shore. He kept it up till we were fifty yards from them, and then sat down, presenting to them the uncompromising back view of righteous indignation.

I learned the story by degrees; he was still much too angry to want to talk unless to an enemy. During the night our bamboo canoe poles had been taken, and worthless poles of *mirrdi*, the big reed, substituted for them. (The two are barely distinguishable, but the bamboo poles, which are imported, are tough and valuable, while those made from the local reed are worthless and weak.) It had been some phase of this substitution that I had seen when I had woken in the night to see the youth standing naked on the platform, and his nudity had no doubt been designed to suggest that he had but that instant woken from sleep, aroused by the poles slipping down on to him from where they were propped. When the substitution was discovered Thesiger had taxed him with it and received an insolent reply that those battered and crooked reeds were the poles with which he had been entrusted the evening before. Thesiger then boxed his ears, but he kept on protesting his innocence.

Those are the kind of circumstances in which I am perpetually amazed and abashed by other people's unfaltering conviction that they are acting rightly. Had I been Thesiger I should by then have been convinced that I had made a mistake and was beating up the wrong man; the situation, too, would not have been easy to redeem. Thesiger, however, was tormented by no such doubts, and at length the boy had offered to restore the poles.

It took him some time, for he had distributed them among all the neighbouring houses. Each time he returned with one he said that it was the last of which he knew anything, but each time threats had driven him out again until at last the collection was complete. Thesiger had left the house then, and had become immediately engulfed in the hostile crowd where I had glimpsed him.

"We were running quite a big risk, really," he said; "they might easily have turned savage and got out their rifles— and all the time you were wandering about the village taking photographs as if you were a tourist in the Vatican City!"

When all the canoe poles had finally been collected a passenger whom we had carried with us for the past twenty-four hours had reported that his club had been stolen during the night. Thesiger sent Hassan back to tell the tearful youth that unless it were given up at once the Englishman would come back. Without word or demur the boy produced the club from beneath the reed matting on the floor.

"That," said Thesiger, "is what happens when you take their sheikhs away. No village with a sheikh would have dared to try that on. I told you they'd want watching."

We made an hour's journey through flower-choked water-ways in low green marsh, and stopped at another big island village. It was plain to me when we landed that Chahala was dying. She was weak but restless, and inside the house she sought the dark corners between the reed columns and the matting walls. She lay belly downward, breathing fast and in obvious distress. Perhaps something in our huge medicine chest could have saved her, but we thought only of castor oil, for everything she had eaten the night before was still inside her. The oil had little effect, and though she sucked almost automatically from her bottle there was little life in her. I had sat hopelessly beside her for a couple of hours when Thesiger came in from doctoring. "Better get out for a bit," he said. "I'll keep an eye on her. It's hell for you sitting in here all the time, and you can't do her any good. This is your last marsh village, and you may never see another."

I went out, and remembered things that I had wanted to photograph and always postponed. Then I found that the shutter of my camera was broken, and I went back into the house.

We left an hour later. When I felt the warmth of Chahala next to my shirt again I felt a moment's spurious comfort that she would live; but she would not stay there. She climbed out with a strength that surprised me, and stretched herself restlessly on the floor of the canoe, and I spread a handkerchief over my knees to make an awning of shade for her small fevered body. Once she called faintly, the little wild lonely cry that would come from her as she slept, and a few seconds after that I saw a shiver run through her body. I put my hand on her and felt the strange rigidity that comes in the instant following death; then she became limp under my touch.

"She's dead," I said. I said it in Arabic, so that the boys would stop paddling.

Thesiger said "Are you sure?" and the boys stared unbelievingly. "Quite dead?" they asked it again and again. I handed her to Thesiger, the body drooped from his hands like a miniature fur stole. "Yes," he said, "she's dead." He threw the body into the water, and it landed in the brilliant carpet of white and golden flowers and floated on its back with the webbed paws at its sides, as she had been used to sleep when she was alive.

"Come on," said Thesiger, "Ru-hu-Ru-hu!" but the boys sat motionless, staring at the small corpse and at me, and Thesiger grew angry with them before they would move. Amara kept on looking back from the bows until at last we rounded the corner of a green reed-bed and she was out of sight.

The sun shone on the white flowers, the blue kingfishers glinted low over them and the eagles wheeled overhead on the blue sky, but all of these seemed less living for me than Chahala was dead. I told myself that she was only one of thousands like her in these marshes, that are speared with the five-pointed trident, or shot, or taken as cubs to die slowly in more callous captivity, but she was dead and I was desolate. The fault lay with whoever, perhaps more than a million years ago, had first taken up the wild dog cub that clung to the body of its dead dam, and I wondered whether he too had in that half-animal brain been driven by the motives that in me were conscious.

Hubble-bubble

Epilogue

THE journey was over; on the evening of the day that Chahala had died we reached the Tigris at Ezra's Tomb. The sheikh in whose house we stayed was away in Baghdad, and the building was shuttered and deserted but for one old negro retainer. Thesiger, however unsentimental about animals his own outlook, was deeply sympathetic to my abject dejection at the death of Chahala, and I felt it strange that I could have travelled so far alone with one Englishman and known so little of him.

He was returning to Basra only to collect his letters, before leaving to spend the early part of the summer among the pastoral tribes; now he suggested that instead of going back to England I should stay with him. "You'll be able to see another way of life; and," he added, "you can get another otter." I did not need the extra bait; I realised now that I had dreaded returning home, and to remain in Iraq seemed reprieve.

And so it was arranged that we should stay in Basra only long enough to collect and send letters, and leave together after two or three days. But the plan proved as insecure as had earlier projects for travel in Iraq.

From Ezra's Tomb we drove some sixty miles to Basra, and when we reached the Consulate-General we found that Thesiger's letters had arrived but mine had not. I cabled to England, and when, three days later, nothing had happened, I tried to telephone. The call had to be booked twenty-four hours in advance, and could only be arranged for a single hour of the day, an hour during which, owing to the difference in time, no one in London was likely to be available. On the first day the line was out of order; on the second the exchange was closed for a religious holiday. On the third day there was another breakdown. I arranged to join Thesiger at Adb el Nebi's *mudhif* in a week's time, and he left.

Two days before the date of our rendezvous I returned to the Consulate-General late in the afternoon, after several hours' absence, to find that my mail had arrived. I carried it to my bedroom to read, and there squatting on the floor were two marsh Arabs; beside them lay a sack that squirmed from time to time.

They handed me a note from Thesiger. "Here is your otter, a male and weaned. I feel you may want to take it to London—it would be a handful in the *tarada*. It is the one I originally heard of, but the sheikhs were after it, so they said it was dead. Give Ajram a letter to me saying it has arrived safely—he has taken Kathia's place. . . . "

I untied the sack and out of it stepped a small creature quite unlike any otter I had ever seen. He raised to me a blunt face with a black-button nose like a koala bear; then he looked round him and shook his short mole-like fur.

But Mijbil, an otter of a race quite unknown to science, deserves a book to himself; a book that I shall write when my memories of his year with me are less troubled.

Buffalo shelter and house, Eastern Marshes

MORE ABOUT PENGUINS
AND PELICANS

For further information about books available from Penguins please write to Dept EP, Penguin Books Ltd, Harmondsworth, Middlesex UB7 0DA.

In the U.S.A.: For a complete list of books available from Penguins in the United States write to Dept CS, Penguin Books, 625 Madison Avenue, New York, New York 10022.

In Canada: For a complete list of books available from Penguins in Canada write to Penguin Books Canada Ltd, 2801 John Street, Markham, Ontario L3R 1B4.

In Australia: For a complete list of books available from Penguins in Australia write to the Marketing Department, Penguin Books Australia Ltd, P.O. Box 217, Ringwood, Victoria 3134.

In New Zealand: For a complete list of books available from Penguins in New Zealand write to the Marketing Department, Penguin Books (N.Z.) Ltd, P.O. Box 4019, Auckland 10.

A selection

PASSAGES FROM ARABIA DESERTA
C. M. Doughty
Selected by Edward Garnett

Eccentric, redolent with sharply observed life, anecdote, local colour and telling detail, *Arabia Deserta* is not only a Victorian traveller's interpretation of a mysterious – and largely unfathomed – Orient, but also a daring experiment in the use of language at its richest.

'A book so majestic, so vital, of such incomparable beauty of thought, of observation, and of diction as to occupy a place apart' – *Observer*

ONE'S COMPANY
Peter Fleming

Packed with classic incidents – brake-failure on the Trans-Siberian Express, the Eton Boating Song singing lesson in Manchuria – *One's Company* is Peter Fleming's account of his journey to China as Special Correspondent to *The Times* in 1933.

'Original and impressive . . . As a journalist he is modernity itself; as a traveller he has about him an Elizabethan aroma, being both cruel and amused' – Harold Nicolson in the *Daily Telegraph*

AFRICA DANCES
Geoffrey Gorer

Describing his travels through French West Africa, Senegal, French Guinea, the Ivory Coast, Dahomey, the Gold Coast and Nigeria, Geoffrey Gorer's marvellous book vividly recreates an Africa on the point of transition.

'He has made one of the most singular journeys of modern times . . . There are no reservations in this astonishing book. Sex, religion, politics, the negro conception of life contrasted with the white man's, the place of fetish and magic, wrestling, dancing and marriage . . . The result is a book I could not put down' – *Daily Telegraph*